CHRISTMAS

IN

MONTPELIER

CHRISTMAS IN MONTPELIER

F. ROSS PETERSON

Probitas Press
Los Angeles

Published in the United States by
Probitas Press, LLC, Los Angeles
www.probitaspress.com
800.616.8081

PUBLISHER'S CATALOGING-IN-PUBLICATION DATA
Peterson, F. Ross
Christmas in montpelier / Ross Peterson
— First edition

Includes biographical references, glossary and index.
1. Peterson, F. Ross (Frank Ross), 1941 - author. 2. Childhood and youth.
3. Christmas—Anecdotes. 4. Friendship 5. Social life and customs 6. Montpelier
(Idaho, United States)—History, Local—20th century. 7. Teenage boys 8. High
school boys. 9. Missionary—Church of Jesus Christ of Later-day Saints (LDS)
Great Lakes Region, United States.
BISAC: BIOGRAPHY & AUTOBIOGRAPHY / Personal Memoirs. | FAMILY &
RELATIONSHIPS / General. | FAMILY & RELATIONSHIPS / Life Stages / Adolescence.
| FAMILY & RELATIONSHIPS / Friendship. | EDUCATION / Secondary | NONFICTION
/ Religious / Christian / Holidays & Celebrations.
Classification: LCC: F750.22.P48 A5 2020 | DDC: 979.6/033092—dc23

Christmas in Montpelier recalls twelve true stories from the author's youth.
Growing up in Montpelier, Idaho, Ross learns valuable lessons of service,
responsibility, and faith.

ISBN 978-0-9961850-3-5 (print)
ISBN 978-0-9961850-4-2 (eBook)

Cover art: "Four Horse Power"
Courtesy of Robert Duncan
http://www.robertduncanstudios.com

Interior western drawings by Max Peterson
Book Design by Mickey Fryer

ProbitasPress.com | Fax 323-953-9850 | Office/text 800-616-8081
2016 Cummings | Los Angeles, CA 90027
ymaddox@probitaspress.com

10 9 8 7 6 5 4 3 2 1
Printed in the United State of America

Dedicated to my sister and brothers

Clockwise top left: Max (1938 – 2018), Donna Lee (1935 – 2008),
Karl (1934), Ross (1941), Brent (1949), Reed (1946)

Beloved Main Street trees looking west from M Hill, 1950s.

CONTENTS

ACKNOWLEDGMENTS

This project is a labor of love which transcends decades and is based on personal reminiscences and recollections. I owe a debt to my siblings who have prodded my memory, corrected some of my misconceptions, but understood that these stories are mine. I appreciate using some of my brother Max's drawings; he planned to develop more illustrations, but sadly cancer took him in 2018. We also are thrilled to use the Robert Duncan painting as the cover.

Our children, grandchildren, nephews and nieces, thrived on the opportunity to learn details of our youth. They are aware of how dramatically life changes through technology and invention. In our lives, Christmas has been a constant, even though our economic and geographic circumstances created intriguing variations.

When I decided to compile these Christmas stories about growing up in rural Idaho during the 1940s and 1950s, I was encouraged by many friends who shared those experiences. Yvonne and Lee Roderick helped in the preparation for publication. Their professionalism, care, and devotion to the topic encouraged me. Lisa Godfrey, a beloved friend and former student, took the time to help edit, organize, and reformat the text. She noticed many problems that come from my assuming a reader knows my thoughts. Grandson Anthony Peterson also gave the stories a close rereading and helped clarify the relevance of the message.

Whenever I write, the presence of my high school English teacher, Lewis Munk, is in my head. Simply put, he proselytized the virtue of the written word. We learned by reading the masters. Mr. Munk then taught us the basics and allowed us to write, rewrite, and for good measure, start all over again. He epitomized the many devoted teachers who have guided me throughout my career at all levels.

I love my hometown and its people. Some of the toughest, kindest, meanest, forgiving, and loving of God's human creations roamed those streets and I learned from all of them. Their children were my friends and our fondness grows as time passes.

Though very different now, Montpelier is still home. When I visit, I frequently stop by the high school, gymnasium, tabernacle, and my church, which are nostalgic magnets.

Most importantly, I married a Montpelier native and that fact has helped considerably on this project. Kay knows the truth and she understands that we live life in the long run. Her love, patience, support, and passion for Montpelier inspire me.

Main Street looking east

A frosted tree after a Montpelier fog.
Courtesy of Linda Stephens Walker

INTRODUCTION

In November 1999 my friend and former student, John R. Miller, called and invited me to a family and friends Christmas party at his home in Park City, Utah. I accepted. Then he added, "Will you please bring your favorite Christmas story and read it to the group?" I agreed. Obviously my favorite story was authored by Luke with a little Matthew added in. After visiting with my older brother Max I decided to write something from our youth. The result was the first story included in this collection. I have written a Christmas story every year since.

Included in this edition are stories that relate to Christmases in my hometown, Montpelier, Bear Lake County, Idaho. I can say with complete honesty that all the stories are based on actual events, but I placed some in a Christmas setting to fulfill the tradition requested by our grandchildren and many friends.

When I left for college in the fall of 1959, my parents said that upon graduation, I was welcome to come back to Bear Lake. But the farm could not support more than one family at best. Of five brothers and a sister, I may have had the least interest in farming. It was unlikely that I would ever go back. My brother Reed is the only one who did. He has devoted his life to making Montpelier a good and decent place as mayor, councilman, and booster. He and his family live in our family home.

Once I started to write about Christmas, Montpelier was always somewhere in the forefront of my mind. The town, nestled on the Oregon Trail in Bear Lake Valley was founded in 1864 by Mormon pioneers. At nearly 6,000 feet elevation, the beautiful valley is not an agricultural paradise. The growing season averages less than ninety days, yet most of the early settlers did farm by acquiring homesteads from the public domain.

In the early 1880s the valley got a tremendous economic boost when the Union Pacific Railroad built the Oregon Short Line, as a shortcut from the Midwest to Portland. Railroaders were often referred to as "gentiles" and primarily lived on the west side of town. Feelings were so intense between Mormons and gentiles that for a brief time a large fence was constructed through the middle of town from north to south. Mormons patronized uptown Mormon-owned stores and "Gentiles" supported their stores, which lined Main Street near the railroad. After Idaho's statehood in 1890, public education helped break down local barriers.

Montpelier was a great place to learn life's lessons. During my childhood there were fewer than 3,000 citizens in the city that served as an economic center for Bear Lake County because of the Union Pacific and the intersection of U.S. Highways 30 North and 89. Montpelier was amazingly alive with cafes, hotels, barber shops, motels, grocers, and many service stations.

Located on Main Street were many chains, such as J. C. Penney, M. H. King, OP Skaggs, Safeway, and Western Auto. Chevrolet, Ford, Chrysler, Pontiac, Studebaker, and for a brief time Kaiser, all had dealerships. The Rich Theater showed the latest movies and, on Saturdays, children's matinees for nine cents. Two grain elevators sat alongside the railroad tracks and shipped barley or wheat to mills in Ogden, Utah. San Francisco Chemical, which operated phosphate mines at various locations in the Bear River Range, had an office in town.

The county was divided into two high schools, Fielding in Paris, and Montpelier High, built with federal dollars during the New Deal. Montpelier had two grade schools, Washington and Lincoln. Our family lived east of Main and all went to the Washington School, built around 1900. It was located on Fourth Street, which also included the high school football field, track and field facilities, an open irrigation ditch, and in the winter, an ice skating rink. Fire drills consisted of the fourth, fifth, and six graders jumping into an open canvas chute from the second floor and sliding toward teachers or large boys who were holding the bottom near the ground.

The junior high school had been the original Montpelier High School. It also had two stories. In junior high, children from Bern, Nounan, and Bennington joined us. In addition, for high school, were those from Georgetown and Geneva. When my family moved into a new home on Fifth Street in 1948, we were located less than a block and a half from any of the three schools we attended. During grade school, if you played in the band, you walked to the high school during the last period. For two years Jerry Bissegger, Charles Sorensen, and I walked from the Washington school to the High school and, fooling around, never got there on time.

Three characteristics of a typical Mormon village need explaining. One is that the square blocks were surveyed and usually numbered from a main street. In Montpelier, Main Street ran from the railroad tracks on the west to the base of "M" Hill on the east. It was approximately twelve blocks or a mile and a half long.

Second, the town was divided into LDS wards—individual congregations—based on population within so many square blocks. Montpelier had four wards.

The children who went to school with us often went to the same ward as well. When we started junior high school, a pack of friends was well defined. Children of a different faith, and there were never many, had options with the Catholic church or the Community congregation, but often joined us for Boy Scouts or other social programs. The third typical characteristic was that everyone knew everybody and the village could be nurturing or tough, depending on how one behaved.

As much as the town, the valley, the buildings, the streets, and the farm shaped me, it is really the people who never leave my thoughts. My classmates from first grade through high school, and other friends with whom we shared tragedies, successes, and so many experiences, are still friends.

When I remember all that my family did to sacrifice for each other, my thoughts include neighbors and friends. The schools and the church gave us exceptional teachers and mentors who helped with discipline, but more importantly opened our eyes to possibilities. Some appear in these stories and others do not, but those housewives, teachers, farmers, veterans, postal clerks, and carpenters who taught and inspired me are a constant reminder of service. I have tried to adapt those many lessons for my children and students.

I wrote these memories to introduce my children and grandchildren to my parents, who died in 1975 and 1976 before they were really known by their extensive offspring. Raymond and Zora Peterson never lived outside that beautiful high-mountain valley during forty-one years of marriage. They married during the Great Depression and lived the sacrifice of World War II, teaching us that education and hard work are necessities. Every day I realize the impact of their determination to serve others.

They provided us the opportunity to choose our destiny. For that and so much more, I am eternally grateful.

Sheep camp like Tweedy's

1
A Tweedy Christmas

Christmas Eve again. The same routine— delivering plates of goodies, or a Santa Claus candle, or a green and red towel to all the neighbors. You often met those same neighbors bringing their goodies, candles, or towels. It is great, but every year I complain a little. Every year I am reminded of giving and service, so I do my duty and make all of the obligatory exchanges. Tradition. How did my wife adopt a tradition of my mother's? Ah, my mother— every year another Christmas project.

On impulse, I reached for the phone and called my older brother Max.

"Do you remember the Ed Tweedy Christmas?"

"Sure do! How could I ever forget it? It was 1945, the year the war ended. The year we about lost our whole herd to the cold."

As we talked, the memories came flooding back of that long ago Christmas.

It seems that it was always colder and the snow piled higher every winter when we were young. At least when it snowed it was a little warmer. It is true that there are few colder places in the lower forty-eight states than the Bear Lake Valley in southeastern Idaho. This was especially true in the late 1940s.

When Dad finished milking the cows, straining the milk, and pouring it into the galvanized steel ten-gallon cans, he called to us. "Bundle up—it's Christmas Eve—we've got packages to deliver. I'll go start the car."

Mother had gathered what seemed like hundreds of half-bushel woven wooden slat fruit baskets filled with a variety of fresh fruit, home canned goods, loaves of freshly baked bread, and knitted mittens, hats, or scarves. We have remembered since where we got all that fresh fruit in the winter. Dad worked for Pacific Fruit Express railway, keeping produce from spoiling in the summer and freezing in winter. They allowed employees to take home produce that was overly ripe. Each basket was carefully labeled. We moved the baskets next to the door near the large cast-iron stove, which both heated the house and cooked our meals.

In a few minutes Dad came into the room with a gust of blowing snow. "Darn car won't start! We'll have to hook up the team." Telling my oldest brother, Karl, to come help him, he told the other two of us to arrange the baskets in the best order for delivery. As we watched the blizzard through the window, we hoped that Dad would say "maybe tomorrow" or "when the storm ends," but instead, he went to the barn to hook up Belle and Mark to an old box sleigh with wooden runners. The sleigh had high plank sides and was used to haul newborn lambs and their mothers into the protected sheds during lambing season.

A short time later we heard the jingle of the harness bells, and Dad gave his "Get Moving!" whistle. He had filled the sleigh with hay and we hurriedly piled in with all of the baskets. Then he told Karl and Max to grab their sleighs and some ropes. The cold wind forced us deep down into the hay.

Suddenly Mother appeared at the doorway and shouted "Did you get Tweedy's basket?" Tweedy's!!! We shuddered. Ed Tweedy lived about three miles west of town in a canvas-covered sheep camp. He had at least five of the meanest dogs in captivity, whose teeth were always threatening.

"Why Tweedy?" No one answered. Mother handed Dad a big flour sack full of who knows what. "Put it last," he said.

As we moved from home to home, Dad made the three of us carry the baskets to the older couples and widows, most of whom had good cause to hate us, due to our raiding gardens, stealing apples, tearing out irrigation dams, chasing their chickens, or whatever. We smiled and wished them Merry Christmas, knowing that next summer would witness a return to the mischief that led many to refer to us with a series of words usually reserved for milk cows. When we went to families with children, Dad took the baskets in—even to some of our friends.

"Hey, Dad, I want to see Grant," I said.

"No, I'll do it."

"That's not fair—we had to go to Mrs. Holmes' house and she tried to kill us last summer with a rake! Come on, Dad, let us take them in," we persisted.

He thought for a moment and then shook his head. "Sometimes folks don't like to show they don't have much—so just be quiet. I make the rules."

Finished delivering baskets in town, Dad turned the team west, straight down Main Street. The road was divided, and in the median were giant blue spruce trees with large Christmas lights and so much snow you could barely see the filtered glow from the bulbs. Main Street was deserted as the team pulled the sleigh across the Union Pacific Railroad tracks, past the roundhouse and toward the snow-covered west fields. We burrowed deeper into the hay. Dad muttered, "The car couldn't make it anyway." Then he began to sing some of his western songs.

"We don't have much either," volunteered Max from the hay.

'Yeah," I added. "We only get two gifts. Are we poor?"

"Hey, Dad, will someone drop something off at our house?"

"Maybe Santa Claus," he answered.

The chatter continued as we moved toward Ed Tweedy's sheep camp. We could now see, leaning against the canvas cover of his camp, the legendary bicycle he rode to town – hoses for tires, tied on with wire, a gunnysack seat, and an air horn on the handlebars. As we approached, the dogs began to bark, his mule brayed, and then Tweedy appeared at the door with his shotgun.

"It's Raymond, Ed. Me and the boys."

"What do you want?"

"Brought you some things. It's Christmas."

"I'm fine—don't need nothin."

"Ed, if I don't give you these, *we* won't get a Christmas! Can we come in?"

"Dad, don't ask!" Karl muttered, mostly to himself (we'd been here before). "It stinks and the dogs nip at you and we'll never get home for Christmas." Max whispered, to no avail, "Give him the flour sack and let's go!"

Tweedy slowly moved aside, motioning us in. Three boys, two men, and five wet dogs squeezed around a tiny pot-bellied stove in the middle of the camp wagon. No one could move. Ed Tweedy had beady eyes beneath a full, gray beard, brushes for eyebrows, no teeth, and a limited but profane vocabulary. He always smoked a pipe but in no way did he remind us of Santa Claus. This place was so filthy that all the elves in the world could not restore order. Tonight, though, at least it was very warm.

Dad handed Tweedy the flour sack and the old man slowly looked at each item which Mother and my sister had put in the bag – a tin of coffee, some flour, a dozen eggs, sugar, bottled fruit, a few apples, oranges, and bananas. There were also bones for the dogs, matches, and a knitted stocking cap. We boys sat looking in total silence as Tweedy muttered "thanks" and poured a cup of the blackest coffee I had ever seen for my Dad. As Dad sipped it, Tweedy shifted his attention to us.

"You boys think you are the Wise Men? Well, I ain't no baby Jesus. Can't do much about His being born—do even less about His dying—just live what he taught. I can't do it, won't do it, but won't do you no harm."

He looked at each of us. Then, reaching under his cot, he pulled out a box and gave each of us a hand-carved willow whistle with the dried bark tied on by thread. Dad rose.

"Thanks Ed. Merry Christmas!"

Before we climbed back onto the sleigh, Dad threw all the hay toward Ed's mule, one more small Christmas gift. As we pulled away the dogs licked us and yapped, and we could see Tweedy silhouetted through the canvas.

Karl and Max tied their sleds to the back of the large sleigh and rode all the way back to the railroad tracks.

Belle and Mark knew we were headed for the barn as we turned toward home, at times their trot shifting to a gentle lope. We felt good about our deeds of deliverance. Dad let us out at the house before he took the team to the barn. The horses were rewarded by having their harnesses removed and a fresh drink of water and some oats.

We gathered around the kitchen stove, took turns running to the outhouse, and then listened as Mother read the story of Jesus' birth. Our sister Donna Lee had strung popcorn which circled the tree and we made red and green paper chains. Then we threw tinsel icicles everywhere. We took one more peek under the tree to see if the number of presents had increased. No luck. The radio reported a Santa Claus sighting somewhere over Canada.

It was late, the day had been long, and we raced for the bed, which the three of us shared, kicking our legs under the quilts to warm up the bedding. "Say your prayers," Mother reminded, so out and in again. Time elapsed: less than fifteen seconds.

1945 had been a great year because the war ended and so many friends and neighbors returned home. However, Mother reminded us of families that had lost a child, a husband, or a father in the war. This Christmas proved tragically memorable for other reasons too. Up before dawn, we tried and tried to get our parents moving. We had to act fast before Dad went out to milk, or to hook up the team to feed the cattle, or to try to start the car. Soon we were all in full scream!

We each received two wrapped gifts plus some games from Santa. For each boy there was a sailor hat, brought back by Uncle Leon from the Navy, and some article of clothing. My sister received a beautiful new dress. For me, there was a handcrafted wooden jeep about 12-inches long. Its wheels moved perfectly over the linoleum floor and everything was so nice.

No one noticed the cold, or even the warmth once the fire got going, or that Dad had given my brothers the ultimate gift by slipping out to do the chores alone. Life was good as all the children played on the new Chinese Checkers board with our old marbles. Dad came back in time to cook his famous flapjacks for breakfast.

Suddenly there was a knock at the door. Dad answered—it was the County Sheriff. "Ray, can I talk to you and Zora?" We were ushered into the bedroom, behind a closed door, as they sat around the table, but our ears could hear through the paper-thin walls.

"Fire in Montana . . . Baby burned and died. Uncle Walt badly burned . . . House destroyed. Lost everything . . . They need you!"

"We'll go today. Help me start the car. Zora, tell the children."

Mother sobbed as she told the tragic story. Then her blue eyes lit up and maybe even twinkled. "You can help so much. Your cousins lost their entire Christmas. Actually, everything they own." Suddenly the pain became very personal. She led us down a path where there was only one answer. "You decide what you want us to take to your cousins."

Slowly, Donna Lee re-wrapped her new dress, went to the dresser drawer and pulled out other things. There were two girl cousins and a boy about my age. We did the same— clothes, sailor hats, and games. The jeep, however, just seemed like it should stay. It was a Santa gift, no wrapping paper. Maybe if it kind of got shoved under a bed and forgotten. "Just think of what they would really like, not what they need." Case closed. The perfect wooden jeep that rolled so straight was headed north.

Our parents packed the car, at the same time giving a thousand instructions on who was to do what, how to do it, and what to do if the pipe to the well froze, and how to separate the milk, and on and on.

Ed Tweedy rode up on his mule, followed by the dogs. He had the flour sack and a few other things. It seems he had ridden into town and heard the story. (Privacy does not exist in a small town.) Tweedy gestured my Dad over. He returned our gifts and also gave Dad a new blanket that he had bought himself. Then the old man said to us, "Just live it."

Dad and Mother drove away toward Montana. We just sat, each with our own thoughts. In the minds of children, the totality of the Christmas message was not clear. The Savior was born, He had died, and we could try to live as He had taught. The tragedy confused us and did not seem to fit the season.

Today, decades later, Max's recollection of all this had brought back a thousand memories of my own. Saying goodbye to my brother, I hung up the phone. Then the words of the Savior echoed in my mind.

"Inasmuch as ye have done it unto one of the least of these, my brethren, ye have done it unto me."

Now a father myself, I moved quickly to fill my truck with the plates of goodies, towels, candles, and my own three sons, and headed out into the night to give greetings to our neighbors. Then we went to the grocery store and bought fruit, flour, and coffee, in honor of Tweedy, to add to our load and took it all to the Homeless Shelter.

CARROT BAIT (Maybe Tease)
JAN. 13, 2013
Max Peterson

2

The Ranching Routine

Farm life is a continual routine, but every hour within the routine is different. Something can break down; in fact, something will break down. In the cold, harsh winter, it isn't that things break down as much as it is the fact that calving season is December and January. Keeping the newborn calves alive is a constant worry.

On a beautiful, clear pre-Christmas morning, Kay and I walked to the lower ranch at Deep Springs College, in the high desert of eastern California. We wanted to check on the first two of this year's crop of new calves, which had been born in the past few days.

We found Iris Pope sitting in her truck with binoculars focused on a fence line a couple hundred yards away. Her routine was to monitor fifty heifers as they delivered their first calves. We quietly watched as a young cow separated herself from the herd and with tail poised at an awkward angle and hips swaying, slowly dropped into a spot along the fence. Even from a distance, the binoculars allowed us to see her ribs heave as she panted, and then she stopped. We watched, almost holding our breath, as the young cow stood up and began to lick her newborn calf.

Slowly we drove across the alfalfa field. This cow's motherly instincts were instantly evident, and she nudged her little one from side to side as she cleaned up the tiny brockle-faced red and white calf. Suddenly my mind was flooded with a scene that happened over a half-century ago and seven hundred miles away.

Dad's winter routine in December 1946 depended on whether he worked swing shift (4 p.m. to midnight) or graveyard (midnight to 8 a.m.) for the Pacific Fruit Express. Most farmers in Bear Lake County, Idaho had to have another job in order to pay for their losses on the farm. Dad went to work for the PFE during World War II and had only enough seniority to work about six months a year lighting charcoal heaters or icing railroad cars. He belonged to a railroad union brotherhood, was paid twice a month, and voted for any and every Democrat.

My mother worked hard, riding herd on five children and homemaking in a two-bedroom house without running water or indoor plumbing. During the fall she canned everything she could acquire in shiny two-quart Kerr or Mason jars. For our meat supply, Dad slaughtered a pig, shot a deer, slit a sheep's throat, or randomly dispatched chickens and domestic rabbits.

These seasonal tasks were like alarm clocks ringing in their heads. The routine kicked into gear early every day. Survival depended on maintaining the routine that supplied daily milk, bread, and meat for us, our neighbors, extended family, and those "less fortunate." The cornerstone of our farm existence was really three or four cows (milked twice daily), a few draft horses, and several beef cattle. If Dad worked swing shift, he came home after midnight to a very cold house. The fire in both the kitchen and living room stoves had long turned to glowing embers and then to cold gray ash.

Every morning at 6 a.m. Dad got up and walked past the outhouse, chicken coop, and pig pen to the barn. His routine had begun. As soon as he opened the barn door, the nearly frozen cows hustled in and went immediately to each one's own stanchion for milking. The cows chomped on hay and chewed grain while Dad milked them. I was always amazed that his left hand, minus most of a thumb and three fingers (from a boyhood accident), stripped milk from the teats as easily as the right hand.

Dad usually left his team of horses in the barn overnight, although the wind still sliced through the cracks between the weathered wallboards. Even so, the barn was much warmer than the barnyard, which was filled with frozen manure, including a large pile thrown from inside the barn.

As a child I'd ask Dad why the frosty breath from the cow's mouth was cold and the greenish-brown deposit, as it hit the shallow trench behind the cow, steamed with warmth? He'd just chuckle. The cow's milk was also warm. Occasionally, Dad squirted some directly into my mouth, missing deliberately every once in awhile, and sending some up my nose or into my eyes. After milking, cleaning the barn, and letting the cows out, he poured the milk through the strainer into a ten-gallon steel can.

Then, at home, Mother ran the separator, later using the cream for a variety of cooking delights. I was five that winter, and I followed Dad everywhere. As soon as we left the barn, we went to the house for breakfast. Leaving our boots on the enclosed back porch, we huddled around the huge cast-iron stove, eating hot oatmeal and flapjacks along with warm milk. Life was good before school became a routine of its own.

After eating, Dad moved a pot of boiling water off the stove and took it behind the house to pour it on the hand pump above the well.

Sometimes he had to dig the snow away, but new snow usually meant the air was warmer. Once the pump thawed, Dad pumped enough water for Mother's daily needs. On Saturday, he pumped and pumped until he had enough to fill a good-sized galvanized tub for our weekly baths, youngest to oldest, with the water heated on the stove.

At this point in the routine, I invariably started begging Dad to let me go with him. "It's too cold," he'd say. And I would counter with, "I could help." He would finally say, "All right, you can go, but if you cry again, I'll leave you in a haystack!" I promised him I'd be big; however, I usually got so cold that I started to cry and he would say, "Never again!" That is, until next time. Idaho did not have Kindergarten so we had this discussion every day.

He was mine for the day. Mother bundled me in snow pants, rubber boots, a hand-me-down coat, scarf, and a hat with ear flaps to tie under my chin. Then I would without fail say, "I gotta go pee!" By now Dad had the team harnessed, hooked to the sleigh, with manure piled high in the sleigh bed.

The two-seat outhouse was my least favorite place. It stunk in the summer, and in the winter, frozen wood splinters made for a terrible seat. Then there was those two seats. I never understood why or how two people could sit comfortably side by side and grunt or sigh away.

Of course, with three layers of clothing on and having to disrobe to sit down, the situation was really less than amusing. But I knew it would be four or five hours until I had another opportunity to go, and Dad was waiting with a sleigh full of manure.

The trip to the farm was about four miles, with the wind blowing from the west right into our faces. It was just me and Dad and he sang and hummed and whistled at his team. Before Dad left for work, he always checked the Union Pacific schedule to see when freight trains might block the road to our farm. He hated being held up at the crossing. Once we got to our land, he hooked the reins to the front of the hay rack and pitchforked the manure off the back of the sleigh next to the ground where he had spread it the day before. He usually commented on the varying virtues of cow, horse, chicken, and pig poop as fertilizer.

When the rack was empty, Dad went to a haystack, climbed up, and tossed alfalfa down to refill the hay rack. He then spread the hay near where he had just deposited the manure. The cattle followed the sleigh until the hay was gone. Next, he guided the team to the Bear River. Jumping from the sleigh and grabbing an axe, he walked out onto the ice to chop a couple of watering holes for the cattle. The holes were fairly small so that a calf could not fall through into the stream. This task completed, he returned to the haystack and filled the rack with hay, burying me to my neck in the process. The hay inside the stack was warm and the trip home much more pleasant.

Every day all winter long, Dad followed that routine. If he worked graveyard, my older brothers milked, and they also helped on weekends, but for five days, Dad was mine—as long as I did not cry. His teams of horses were well trained. A couple of years later, my younger brother Reed fell off, landing near the sleigh's runner. When Dad yelled "Whoa," Bud and Babe stopped on a dime. A nearby railroader ran over and pulled Reed out from under the sleigh.

The Friday before Christmas 1946, the last day before school break and my last day with Dad alone for awhile, the two of us were in the middle of the routine at the ranch when he suddenly stopped. He turned and stared at the cattle following the sleigh. The gentle snowfall made visibility poor, but he quickly scanned the field and willows.

"Where's that damn black-baldy heifer?" he muttered to himself. I rose to my tiptoes as if to help, but saw nothing. Moving swiftly, Dad unloaded the hay, went to the stack yard, loaded the hay to take home, and drove the team to a shed near a bend in the Bear River. He caught Mark, a gray gelding, and grabbed the axe and a rope. He told me to stay buried and warm in the hay. Dad jumped onto Mark's bare back and rode into the willows.

From the perspective of a five-year-old, Dad was gone forever. It stopped snowing and the wind started to howl. The team of horses, unhitched and tied to a fence, stood still, hunched against the wind, pawing at the snow beneath their feet. There was no way I could survive, Dad was lost, the team was unhitched, and no one could find us. Maybe I could ride one of the work horses and they would know the way home. But I knew I could not leave Dad. Panic set in. I broke my promise and started to cry.

Suddenly I heard Dad yell my name. I scrambled out of the hay to see an amazing sight. Straddling the horse in front of Dad was a tiny red newborn calf. Behind Mark came the mother heifer, dragged by a lariat with one end made into a makeshift halter. The calf looked almost lifeless as the cow followed them into the open shed where Dad tried to get the calf to suck. The little fellow could not stand and the mother cow only looked more confused. I tried to figure out how a black-baldy could have a red calf. (Its mother was a black and white Holstein, its father a red Hereford.) Later I became aware of what it meant when it was time to "borrow" the nearest bull.

Dad milked onto his fingers and then stuck his fingers into the tiny mouth. Following this futile trial, he jumped to his feet and carried the calf to the sleigh, where he buried it with me in the hay. He turned Mark loose, hooked up the team, tied the cow to the back of the sleigh and took off for town. As he drove, Dad kept up a constant stream of instructions.

"Keep him warm, little man."

"Rub him. How's he doing?"

"Keep his nose open."

"Squeeze him a little. Rub him again."

Twice Dad stopped, milked onto his fingers, and let the calf suck a little. Holding the little guy up to his mother's teat failed to get him nourished.

As we crossed the railroad tracks onto a plowed road, Dad yelled for joy.

There were Mother, Karl, and Max in the 1942 Ford. No cell phones, no four-wheel drives, just Mother's intuition. Fearing trouble because it was getting near Dad's work time, she drove to the grade school and picked up Donna Lee to tend Reed. Then she retrieved the other boys, and came looking. We had no idea it was nearly four o'clock. Mother was a notoriously bad driver, but never were we happier to see her behind the steering wheel.

I jumped into the warm car as Dad gave my older brothers instructions about the cow, the calf, the horses, milking, and other chores. Karl drove the team and Max cradled the calf. Mother and I dropped Dad off for work at the freight station on the far west end of Main Street.

Mother was magnificent. By the time Karl drove the team into the corral behind our house, Mother had prepared a tiny crib with straw behind the warm kitchen stove. She had readied a bum-lamb bottle, nipple and all, and had hot chocolate ready for everyone. Karl milked the heifer and brought the bucket of milk into the house. Max carried the calf in. We all watched in awe as Mother taught the tiny animal to drink. Donna Lee took over the care of the calf as the older brothers left to do the evening milking. The little calf stayed in the house until after Christmas.

We never talked about it much, but Christmas was different that year. We had a calf in a manger in the house and everyone cared. Christmas still meant oranges, peanuts, and hardtack in little brown paper bags from the Santa downtown on Main Street; the simple gifts of clothes, the games of Rook and Pit, and always the chores—the routine—where every day there was something new.

Christmas was always a pleasant interlude in the routine. One of the treasures of life is memory. And when the birth of a Christmas calf at Deep Springs in 2004 triggered the recollection of a calf born at Christmastime in 1946, it was a reminder that the birth of a child in Bethlehem was a memory to treasure and was certainly not routine.

Santa's Sheep (*clockwise from top left*)
Grant Messerly, Boyd George, Roger Aland,
Calvin Burgoyne, Ross Peterson, George Irving,
Dick Grunig, Bob Wigington, 1949

3
Santa's Sheep

Grant Messerly is definitely his father's son. He looks, talks, and acts just like Eddie. Grant was large, the youngest of three sons and just three days older than me.

As my thoughts turned to his dad, I wondered if Grant too would one day play Santa Claus. Certainly his laugh is the same. We could not stack loose hay like our dads did, or do a lot of other things. The Messerlys' farm was adjacent to ours and we shared some of everything. Big Eddie Messerly was one fine, authentic Santa Claus, but the Christmas of 1948 he had an attitude.

Of course, during the winter of 1948-49 almost everyone had a pretty bad attitude. There was so much snow and so little work available. When Santa came to town two days after Thanksgiving and stopped to deliver candy in front of the Rich Theater, there were already mounds of snow piled in the middle of Main Street. The tiny brown paper bags of hardtack, gumdrops, a few cheap chocolates, and peanuts seemed worth the long wait in line in spite of the freezing cold. The town Santa never questioned you in late November. He just handed out candy.

But the Santa who came to the church Christmas party drilled you about "naughty and nice" the Saturday before Christmas. By age seven, with older siblings, you figured out a few things about apprentice Santas and big elves, but the desire to believe remained powerful. Even if you had seriously misbehaved.

Second-graders are a pretty rowdy group during normal times, but as Christmas approached, our level of scholarly or religious endeavor diminished by the anticipation that surrounded Christmas. I think that Christmas also increased tensions during difficult economic times.

When I look at the picture of Mrs. Marie Bridge's second-grade class at Washington Elementary School, I am struck by distinct images—the appearance of poverty in both clothes and countenances—especially among the nine boys and one girl of the class who were also members of the LDS Third Ward. We all needed Santa Claus and Christmas in 1948, but our collective behavior earned us Santa with an attitude.

The problem was not school per se. Yes, recess caused numerous disasters, primarily because the teeter totters, merry-go-round, and monkey bars were set in ground as hard as concrete. When a child was bounced or fell off, broken bones resulted with frightening frequency. However, the real cause for concern was Primary meeting, held every Thursday immediately following school, at the old Third Ward church building.

After being cooped up in school for six or seven hours, two recesses which usually involved snowball fights or arguments over games, and post-school snacks, children went directly to the church to learn about Jesus and the Prophets. There were no men at Primary. Almost all the children went, even the ones who never came to church on Sundays. It was low-cost, latch-key care. Reverence did not seem to be a viable choice, especially as Christmas neared.

Second-grade is a crucial time in the LDS Church because everyone begins the year at age seven, but as the year progresses and children turn eight, they are baptized. Now if you turned seven in September like Grant Messerly, Calvin Burgoyne, and me, that meant you had an entire year of repentance, baptism, and the Holy Ghost drummed into your head before baptism. When Charles Sorenson and Boyd George were baptized in the fall, we failed to observe any distinct increase in righteousness. Besides, if your birthday was late and your sins were washed away at age eight with baptism, why rush into a new level of expectation?

There were other problems with the system that puzzled me. We had one Primary teacher, Virginia Hymas, whose husband Denzil was deaf and usually turned off his hearing aids, so she just yelled. She screamed all the time. Consequently, the initial level of noise in the classroom was intense.

We needed three teachers, not one, and if anyone had been inspired they would have called Norma Wigington, Bob's mother, because she had no qualms about backhanding any of us. LaPriel Irving was another option. I had seen her dropkick her son, George, into the next county. (I've forgiven her because she was a Democrat who sent me Idaho absentee ballots every election until she died.) Neither Dick Grunig nor Boyd George had a mom, and Gertrude Sorensen, Ruth Messerly, Louise Burgoyne, and my mother already had Primary callings.

Anyway, Mrs. Hymas and Rosanna Coombs, the only girl in class, were pitted against demons unleashed. There is little need to go into specifics, but suffice it to say that almost every week Rosanna and Mrs. Hymas broke into tears and left early. Then Gertrude Sorensen and Louise Burgoyne, after stern threats, piled us into their cars and took us to the homes of the saddened where we individually apologized and humbly promised to cease and desist. Two weeks later the routine was repeated. The Bishop chastised, his counselor cajoled, and our parents responded. Finally Mrs. Hymas quit amidst screams and sobs and Rosanna's parents decided she could no longer associate with us, and she stopped coming to our Primary.

As Christmas approached, the crisis deepened. Every ward had a Christmas pageant in which the Primary children played the various animals and characters depicted in the nativity reenactment. Two weeks before the production, our group was passed over as angels again and the nine boys received the assignment to be sheep. All of the parents, teachers, other adults, and the older children became literal and figurative shepherds. The band of nine was to be controlled at all costs.

Rosanna was coaxed back to sing part of "While Shepherds Watched Their Flock," and rehearsals began. To everyone's surprise, the flock maintained near perfect behavior during the practices. The odds against us were so great that an occasional chorus of "baa, baa, baa" was all we dared try. Little did we know that some of our dads and even Santa Claus himself had hatched their own conspiracy against us. Well, really, for us.

The church was a tiny hall with no permanent pews or benches. At the north end was a slightly elevated stage, maybe just one step up. On Sunday, the stage was where the church leaders sat; on the Saturday night before Christmas it was a theatrical stage. Folding chairs were brought close to the front and almost all of the parents came to watch as the children presented the nativity. Usually, as soon as the performance ended, Santa rolled in and the children lined up to give their final requests and get another brown paper bag of hardtack, gumdrops, cheap chocolates, and peanuts. On a good year, an orange might be found at the bottom of the bag. This year no orange.

In 1948 it snowed a lot that Saturday. By the time we walked to the church, there was a fresh foot of snow piled on what had come earlier. The snow banks beside the cars were well over six feet high. As the sheep were herded into the church kitchen to be dressed and lectured, a fight broke out between Boyd and Dick. Boyd had picked on Calvin because his dad had a good railroad job and Calvin said he wanted an electric train for Christmas. Boyd, whose grandparents had very little means and no work, snapped. Everyone started yelling until the teachers and a couple of parents restored order.

Christmas meant little expectation for some, so no disappointment. For others it meant great hopes and severe discouragement. For me, I was excited because we had moved into a house with central heat and an indoor bathroom, and there was one less person in my bed. For most of us, one gift, maybe two, was our Christmas. Rarely toys, only clothes, boots or mittens were the fate of some. The thought of an electric train was beyond the realm of reality. No wonder we boys were testy and a bit upset.

Finally we were brought out of the kitchen upstairs to the back of the church where shepherds herded us toward the stable on the stage. The white flannel scratched my neck and we let out a few "baas," and made our way to the front as everyone sang.

All the concern left the faces of our parents, teachers, and leaders as the sheep stared into the stable where Paul Sorensen was Joseph, Beverly Keetch was Mary, and Charlotte Burgoyne's new baby was bawling its pre-pacifier eyes out. Then it happened! Just as Rosanna finished her verse, standing tall at the edge of the stage, one of the sheep head-butted her into the second row. She just sprawled, then cried as Mrs. Hymas screamed.

The pageant stopped. The wise men halted in mid-entrance as the sheep were shoved and kicked down the back stairs into a dank basement classroom. It seemed that we had committed an ultimate sin, but no one told who had actually performed the dastardly deed.

Finally we were left alone in the room. The sheep remained sequestered throughout the pageant and missed Santa's entrance and the candy. We suffered in near silence until Roger Aland said he didn't mind missing the candy because he'd just take his little brother's. Bob and I agreed on that possibility. Charles Sorensen, whose dad was in the Bishopric, lamented the lack of a little brother. Grant and Calvin suffered the same fate. Dick, Boyd and George just sat sadly in a corner. It seemed like we were in that room forever. At least we did not reveal the identity of the ram gone astray.

Then my dad and Art Sorensen walked in. I didn't realize that dad knew the church had a basement.

"Take off those sheets, get your coats and boots!"

We obeyed his commands. Then we followed them through the basement to the Bishop's office.

There in the dim light sat Santa Claus.

"Santa wants to talk to you—one at a time." We lined up. There weren't any "Ho, Ho, Hos." I went to the back of the line. Bob went first and it seemed Santa held him very tight, maybe even squeezed him. Santa whispered something. Bob nodded, Santa said more, Bob winced and nodded. Then Santa released him. Bob sat down glumly on the floor in silence. George went next. He could not hear very well and when Santa held him, he tried to squirm away, but Santa's clasp tightened. Finally, George was released as tears formed in his eyes.

The scene was repeated five more times until only Grant Messerly and I remained. Grant went first and Santa about squeezed him into unconsciousness. Grant was the biggest sheep, I was the smallest. As Santa released Grant, he fell onto the huddled boys. My dad left the room as I approached the meanest-looking Santa in history. There was total silence. Why did Dad leave now? Santa grabbed me and pulled me toward his chest. His breath smelled of stale tobacco as he whispered.

"Have you been nice?"

I wanted to say yes, but decided truthfulness may ease his clutch.

"No," I answered.

"Why not?"

"Because."

"Don't give me that 'cause crap!"

I shuddered, but did not dare look at him.

"I'm sorry."

"For what?"

"I'm bad at Primary and school, but I'm not baptized, so I can be forgiven," I blurted out.

"Look at me! I need your help. Will you help me?"

"Yes."

"Now, go get the other boys. All of you, bundle up! Follow me."

Not once did this Santa ask what I wanted. Nor did he give me my candy. We followed him out the back of the church and onto Clay Street. We climbed over the snow piles and he lifted us into a sled covered by a hay rack. My dad had his team hitched to the sleigh—no reindeer, just Bud and Babe, our team of draft horses, with bells jingling from their harness. We sat silently amid the hay piled with numerous presents and food baskets.

As Dad drove around the entire ward, Santa dispatched groups of us to the home of each widow or widower or elderly snowbound couple. Some of us were assigned snow-shovel duty. We totally lost track of time as we made our way from Bleicherts' to Mrs. Follick, to Miss Burgoyne, and on and on.

We sang with Santa and Dad and that is when I thought I recognized Santa's voice. Not the gruff, mean, cantankerous, sullen Santa of the early evening, but the boisterous, melodious strains that I sometimes heard from the front of the pickup when my dad and Eddie Messerly drove home after stacking hay with six boys in the back.

The last stop was at the Coombs' home, next to the church. The house was dark and we started to protest. They weren't elderly or widows or orphans, but Santa silenced us with, "You Promised!" Santa walked with us to the door and we sang until the family opened the door. Rosanna stood in the background as we handed the food and presents for each child. Then Santa handed Rosanna and her brothers some candy as we all yelled, "Merry Christmas." She did not even react, her pain was so deep. For once, we saw and felt it as well.

Dad drove the team to each boy's home, and as they left, Santa thanked them and gave them some packages and food. It was late and we were really tired, but I think each child's face glowed with happiness. Dad and Santa took me home last before they took the team to the barn. I climbed the drift in front of our house and watched the sleigh circle to the north.

The sound of sleigh bells drifted into the night as it moved out of sight. Santa with the attitude had fulfilled his mission. Unfortunately, the Christmas repentance did not last forever, nor even very long, but as a group, we gradually changed. I don't think we were ever quite as bad again.

For all of us, we caught a glimpse of what Christmas could mean that snowy year in our own small corner of the world.

4

Mrs. Scrooge and the Baseballs

"Please, don't make us do that. You know she hates us."

"Can't someone else do it?"

We had a hundred reasons not to cross the street twice a week, break up coal, cut kindling, and throw out the clinkers from Mrs. Holmes's furnace. Our war with her started the first summer after we moved into our new house on North 5th Street in Montpelier. A nasty, cold, bitter winter was not the time to negotiate the summer's battles and atrocities. There could be no truce. Tall, lean, bespectacled and gray, Mrs. Holmes epitomized an evil, uncaring emissary of the devil.

Mother replied with firmness, "Her grandsons are all gone now and she needs someone to help her through the winter."

"Why can't Mr. Burgoyne do it?" Sidney Burgoyne and his brother, Elmer, operated a men's clothing store in downtown Montpelier. Sidney was Mrs. Holmes's son-in-law. The Burgoyne brothers must have slept in their suits; they wore them everywhere. Their children had all left Montpelier and seemed to go to school somewhere forever. They became doctors and lawyers and rarely came back to their hometown.

"Boys," she said, "President Burgoyne is pretty elderly and he works a full day and has been in the stake presidency."

"Church work is no excuse for ignoring your family," I said. That statement was really stupid. Mother's glare reminded me that stubbornness was one of her characteristics.

"We work pretty hard ourselves," said Max. Mother responded with a well-known clicking sound that translated correctly to "You should be ashamed!"

"We have to milk once a day and go to school and help Dad on the weekends and . . ."

"Enough!" she said.

"Mom," I tearfully pulled out all of the emotional stops, "She really hates us. Her cat hates us—it's an attack cat."

"They probably have good reason," Mother responded.

"She's Mrs. Scrooge," I yelled.

Mother won the battle. How could we win the war?

Our troubles with Mrs. Sarah Holmes began in the summer of 1950 when the city decided to create a park between her house and the old junior high school. The city closed one block of Lincoln Street and planted grass everywhere. On the west side of the new park they installed the usual equipment that adults designed to maim children: a merry-go-round, teeter totters, rings, swings, and high and low slippery slides. Under them was gravel, not sawdust or wood chips. Long before OSHA and safety concerns, these units guaranteed that young people suffered.

The east side of the park was all nice new grass, perfect for neighborhood football and baseball. It is only fair to explain that there were plenty of softballs available to us. The problem was that the Boston Braves, New York Yankees, and Brooklyn Dodgers played baseball. The LDS Church had adopted fast-pitch softball as its spiritual game of choice, but we knew God really loved baseball. Thus we tried to play baseball and those smaller, harder balls were scarce. The city fathers neglected to erect a backstop and we tired of chasing errant throws and foul balls into the street.

Consequently our only practical recourse was Mrs. Holmes's fence. That led us directly into prolonged conflict. Every time we started a pick-up game, Mrs. Holmes came out of the side entry of her house, her large, gray, cross-eyed cat at her side. Wearing an apron, leather gloves, and a visor, she carried a long-handled garden rake. She watched and waited. Initially, we thought she loved baseball, but we soon realized her mad mission.

We found a ball and gathered for a game of pick-up one day. The cat pounced on the first foul ball that flew over the fence and into the lilac bush in her yard. The rake-yielding octogenarian deftly pulled the ball back to her and placed it in her apron pocket. The cat kept its eyes on us. We did not have buckets of balls. We only had one. After she raked in the first ball, Max went to the fence and asked for it.

"Get away from my fence," she screamed.

"Go away! Leave me alone!"

"Mrs. Holmes, can we please have the ball?" Max replied.

"Go away!"

That ball was history. As more balls suffered the same fate, we robbed piggy banks and hunted for soda pop bottles to turn in at Hooker's store so we could go down to Thiel and Olsen hardware and buy another ball. By mid-summer we resorted to early-morning bicycle raids behind the Hacienda, a bar and restaurant on North 8th Street. We could put an entire case of bottles on the handlebars and get one dollar per case.

Once we graduated to full cases we had to rotate our business between the larger stores like Jensen's AG and IGA. We had to avoid Teuscher's Market because John Teuscher was the Bishop and we did not want him implicated by receiving stolen goods. Sarah Holmes was rapidly driving us toward a serious life of crime.

After more sad encounters, we responded by placing the on-deck hitters, usually younger boys eager to join our games, at each corner of her fence. When a ball headed in the direction of Mrs. Holmes's yard, they would jump the fence and race her to the ball. She could swing that rake with a vengeance, cursing loudly amid the cat's screeches. Faced with competition for the ball, she and the cat moved quickly.

Although she threatened our lives and we had numerous near misses, we rarely beat her to the ball. She changed tactics and added a high-pressure garden hose to her arsenal. Still we refused to move the diamond away from her fence. Even on Sunday afternoons when "Sister" Holmes should have been napping or reading the scriptures, she'd appear at the crack of the bat or the sound of boys' voices.

We even suspected her of watching us when Max and his friends put me down the junior high school coal chute to open the outside door so we could play basketball. The school district had converted upstairs classrooms into a low-ceiling gym. We'd barely started playing when the police appeared to clear us out. It had to be her. She probably had a spyglass trained on us every waking hour.

One day Max, Reed Stephens, and Dean Wigington forced Bob Wigington and me into boldly entering Burgoyne's store to suggest that Sidney Burgoyne invite his mother-in-law, Mrs. Holmes, to dinner or lunch or breakfast or even to live with them. Sidney shook his head and laughed.

All summer and into the fall, Mrs. Holmes beat us out of baseballs or tennis balls or anything that landed in her yard. Her continual tormenting us caused some serious retaliation on Halloween, but one thing we knew—somewhere in her house or garage or basement were all of those baseballs. That knowledge was what prompted Max to finally tell Mother, "We'll do it. We'll take care of her furnace."

I started whining and complaining, but he ignored me. The next evening while we were milking I began my tirade against Mrs. Holmes, the modern female Scrooge, and then Max explained his plan.

"Look, while we are working in the basement, we can find the baseballs. She has to have them there. This is going to work. No more gathering pop bottles."

That night we went across the street, through the gate and around to the side door where she always appeared with the rake. We knocked loudly and waited. We thought hats with ear flaps or knitted caps might keep her from recognizing our faces as those boys she chased in the summer. Once when Max had gone to collect fast offerings, she said, "Are you one of those bad boys that throws balls in my yard?" "No ma'am," he said as his eyes scoured the living room looking for balls.

"They're going to hell, you know," she said defiantly.

"Oh, they're just playing and having fun," he replied.

"The hell they are. They are going straight to the devil. You tell them. I'll have God waiting to punish the little. . ."

Max interrupted before he heard the self-description. "I need to go. Thanks." He grabbed the brown envelope with her name on it and left. He did not see any baseballs.

Now on a cold winter night we cheerfully returned to the scene of our grief. To be sure, our compassionate service had ulterior motives, but our hearts were pure. "Mrs. Holmes, we're here to take care of the furnace."

The cross-eyed cat hissed a warning.

"Who are you?"

"We're the Petersons from across the street."

"Do you know those boys who throw balls at my house?"

I started to answer, but Max elbowed me into silence. "No, we just moved here."

We followed her down the wooden plank stairs and pulled the strings on the naked light bulbs to light the basement. It was full of wood and there was a closed-in coal bin on the north side. I climbed into the coal bin and started to break the coal into smaller pieces while Max cleaned out the clinkers, cut kindling, and quartered the logs. She never left the basement, watching our every move, the cat at her side.

All through November and December we tried every way to find those balls. We had a friend call on the phone, so one of us could race upstairs to answer and then look under beds, in closets, and in a chest of drawers. Another time we told the ward teachers she wanted them to come at a certain time. We checked the basement and garage and back porch while she was being visited.

Once, Max got her to go upstairs with him. He turned out the lights and I hid in the coal bin. She came back and locked the door to the bin. I had to pile coal against the wall, lift the chute lid with the sledge handle, and climb out, going home covered in coal dust. We tried that again three nights later. After they had left I crawled out and went through every nook and cranny in the basement. Nothing.

Each time we went we tried something new as her trust in us grew. The cat still hissed and yowled, but kept its distance. We visited upstairs, asked to use the toilet, checked under the sink and continued to deny knowing those nasty summer ballplayers. She started calling us when the sidewalk needed shoveling or when some other need required unskilled labor. I broke some lath in order to slide under her front porch, but found nothing but cat crap.

Once Max speculated that the elusive balls had to be in the trunk of her old un-driven 1936 black Buick. She left it parked in a wooden garage behind her home. He got into the garage while I kept her and the cat busy in the basement. Max took out the back seat of the car, crawled into the trunk with a flashlight and came face to face with a nest of mice. Quick exit—no baseballs. We got so desperate that we confided in Dad and our older brother Karl about our quest and welcomed suggestions.

No help was offered.

As the days grew shorter and colder we finally admitted to ourselves that Mrs. Holmes just threw the baseballs away and we needed to stop obsessing over them. She was just protective. She even roamed her backyard when the city flooded the area adjacent to it for a skating rink. One day Sarah Holmes asked us to address her as "Grandma Holmes." As Christmas approached, our hearts softened and we moved on to other pursuits.

On Christmas Eve, shortly after we finished milking, Mrs. Holmes called and said she needed some more wood chopped and coal broken into smaller pieces, so we quickly ran over. She had some hot chocolate and cookies for us. When we finished she thanked us for being so nice, "unlike those naughty summer boys." As we got up to leave, she gave each of us a small, neatly wrapped gift. That was the first time we forgot about looking for baseballs.

We raced home, determined to wait up until Dad came home from his swing shift on the Pacific Fruit Express. We tossed the tiny gifts under the tree, played with Brent and Reed and got them to bed. Reed never slept on Christmas Eve. Mother read the story of Jesus to the rest of us as we waited for Santa Claus and Dad. When Dad came in, he had one box of oranges and another of apples. He and Mother thanked us for helping throughout the year. Karl had had polio that year and was back from the hospital in Pocatello and Donna Lee had survived being quarantined with four younger brothers. This was a very nice Christmas.

On Christmas morning, we thrilled as the Santa toys and family gifts were distributed, unwrapped, and stacked.   Clothes, boots, and books went to the four older children. As the hardwood floor under the tree emptied, someone noticed the tiny boxes from Mrs. Holmes. I quickly ripped off the paper, opened the box, and stared at an old, used baseball. A couple of stitches were broken and the leather seemed hard, maybe waterlogged. Max's box had one too. Dad roared with laughter. Karl nearly choked to death laughing. A note inside Max's box said,

"Thank you for not being like those bad summer boys."

Epilogue: The next summer my dad persuaded the city to build a backstop on the southeast corner of the grass field, so Mrs. Holmes's fence became the right field wall. When she died in 1958 and Harold Phillips, our school principal, purchased her home, I asked him for permission to go through the house and garage before they cleaned out all of her belongings.

I never found a baseball.

Royal Bakery counter, the downtown
gathering place for city leaders in the 1950s

5
Caught in the Act

A dense fog filled Bear Lake Valley on Christmas Eve morning, 1951. As I jogged down Montpelier's Main Street, lighted blue spruce trees in the median glowed softly. I passed City Hall and the Tabernacle, and then cut across Main Street in front of the high school heading toward the town center. At the corner of Eighth Street and Main, there were three service stations—Utoco, Phillips 66, and Texaco. Rich Motor stood on the northwest corner adjacent to the movie theatre of the same name. West of the Texaco station was the Royal Bakery, my destination in the early post-dawn fog.

My search that frigid morning was not in the spirit of the season. I wanted a harmonica, and the local five-and-dime, M. H. King Co., had some for about $2. Truman Rigby, my fifth grade teacher and principal of the Washington School, could play a harmonica, drum, and guitar simultaneously. He may or may not have made great music, but the harmonica, firmly attached to some contraption around his neck, fascinated me. Mr. Rigby promised any student who came back to school after Christmas with a harmonica, he would teach us how to play.

I was not a stranger to music since I shared a trumpet with my brothers in band, but hygienic issues aside, a man needed his own musical instrument. Karl played in the high school band, Max in the junior high, and I in the elementary school version. We played the same trumpet every day and I was last. Our sister, Donna Lee, had her own flute. Since our band director, Wesley Baker, (Montpelier's own "Music Man") had convinced the entire community that music brought salvation to youngsters, we all played.

The main issue for me this Christmas was that I was totally out of money and a harmonica was on no one's radar. In desperation, I went back to all of the delinquent *Deseret News* subscribers on my paper route that had not paid for their paper delivery. I even persuaded my brother Max, a deacon, to take me with him when he was collecting fast offerings for the church. But the good Saints did not like being reminded of their past-due paper account while they were contributing to the Lord's poor.

A few days before Christmas I resorted to my special summer fundraiser of collecting pop bottles and exchanging them at Hooker's Market for 2 cents apiece. Originally this enterprise was left for summer in order to purchase Topps baseball cards at 5 cents a pack, stale, hard bubble gum included. The pop bottle business dwindled when we kept running into adults with gunnysacks and surly countenances who were also gathering. When we found out that Mrs. Hooker paid $1 for a full case of empties—24 bottles, including the case—we made an early run on the Hacienda, a bar/restaurant on Highway 30, about five blocks north of Main Street.

The Hacienda closed late and then no one ever arrived in the mornings before noon, so we helped ourselves to some cases, balanced them on our handlebars and stashed them in Murdock's barn. Every week or so, we'd show up at Hooker's with a full case, split the money and hopefully get some baseball cards that were new and different.

When there was three feet of snow on the ground, dense fog, and piercing cold temperatures, it was difficult to find bottles.

By December 24, I was still a few cents short of the $2. From our summer escapades, I remembered that the Royal Bakery kept their empty soda bottles in a shed across the alley behind the store. Five bottles—one thin dime—

was all I needed. Why I was so driven to get something for myself remains a mystery, but I walked behind the shed, pulled a paper grocery bag from my coat, took off my mitten and reached through a cracked board to feel for the bottles. Unsuccessful, I pushed through clear to my shoulder and finally contacted glass. The neck of the bottle felt just right as I pulled it to the outside.

It was amber—a beer bottle! Darn, what were beer bottles doing in there? The bakery doesn't sell beer. Mrs. Hooker did not offer money for beer bottles. I was just ten years old, so I could not take them to the pool hall for exchange. Regaining composure, I tried my left arm and reached back through the hole.

"Don't move!" a voice screamed as a powerful hand gripped my wrist.

The voice yelled again, "Don't move!"

I froze. He released my arm and I chose not to run.

Freddie Parker had come around the shed, shaking his head. His strong arms were bare and he had a flour-covered apron over his white tee shirt. He wore some type of baker's cap, just like his father-in-law, Mr. Sunderland, who owned the bakery.

"What are you doing? Who are you? What do you want?"

With earmuffs, hat pulled low, three layers of clothing, rubber galoshes, I was disguised. "I was looking for pop bottles, Mr. Parker," I replied.

"So, you know me. Then I must know you. Follow me."

Opening the back door, we were hit with the wonderful scent of baking bread and pastries. As we walked into the bakery I marveled at huge mixing bowls, gigantic ovens and many sacks of flour surrounding the Sunderlands as they baked for everyone's Christmas. I followed Freddie Parker to the retail front of the store where there was a low curving lunch counter with about a dozen stools.

There were display cases for baked goods and against the wall on shelves a variety of other grocery items. The stools were nearly filled with early-morning customers seeking coffee, a roll, and conversation. This was the gathering place for many of the leading citizens of Montpelier, and I stood before them, an unsuccessful thief.

Freddie looked at all of them and then noticed an empty counter space. He glanced at me and said quietly, "Go sit on the stool next to the wall."

He then began pouring coffee, laughing and delivering favorite pastries to his customers without taking a single order. It was a ritual.

After about fifteen minutes, he came to where I was sitting and asked, "Is your dad coming in after he feeds?"

He knew me. That was bad!

"He usually does, but I don't know."

"Well, just stay here. Take your hat and coat off. We'll see."

In many respects, that was my immediate sentence. My dad would be the first to know. I did not fear a physical reprimand from my dad, nor was it embarrassment. It was the guilt of disappointing him. I sat and listened and waited.

Jack Allinger, owner of Allinger's clothing store, asked if anyone had seen the plans for the new high school gymnasium. "We have not had a decent place for the kids to play in over ten years since that old place burned down. It is no wonder that we don't win many games."

Tom Sneddon, owner and operator (with his sons) of Bear Lake Motor Company, the local Ford Motor dealership, added, "We should have asked for some government money long ago." They talked about the war in Korea, Bobby Thomson's home run, who might become President in 1952, and what was the latest happening on the railroad. As the conversation moved back and forth and others chimed in, Freddie refilled the cups, offered a choice of newly baked turnovers, and no one seemed to leave.

I sat. At one point, Mr. Allinger turned and asked me, "Ross, do you need anything? Let me get you some hot chocolate."

"No thanks. I'm waiting for my dad."

Elmer Jensen, the grocer from across the street, added, "Have one of these turnovers."

"No sir, I couldn't," as I shot a quick glance at Freddie. He did not even look my way.

"Now, young feller—a boy doesn't eat, a boy doesn't grow," added Charlie Grimes, a barber.

"No thanks. He'll be here in a minute." I did not like the attention and I feared how and when Freddie would break the news of my crime and destroy my life.

The conversation shifted to baseball, my favorite topic. As I look back, none of those men on the stools at the counter were natives of Bear Lake. They were all businessmen who had cast their lot in this tiny Mormon railroad village in southeastern Idaho. When Eddie Reber, Al Thiel, Harry Nuchols, and Ace Veeley joined the natives in Montpelier, the pattern remained the same. Each loved baseball and had strong opinions about teams and players.

They all sponsored fast-pitch softball teams in a summer recreation league, but their true love was baseball. As they visited about trips to St. Louis, Chicago and New York, I forgot about harmonicas and pop bottles, and for a brief moment, even Christmas. Stan Musial, Willie Mays, Ted Williams, Mickey Mantle, Bob Feller, and Warren Spahn—they had actually seen them! It was unbelievable.

Jack Allinger, who every minute of every day dressed well, noted that, "We need a new ball park. If I had my way, we'd have a baseball field in every town. Yes, sir, we would." Then Ace Veeley, the Montpelier Coal and Lumber owner, added, "That would be a real Christmas—but only if they became Cardinals fans!" Charlie Grimes, a native of Missouri, laughed and said, "They aren't that smart." At that moment Mel Mouritsen, a town policeman, walked in and sat down. I looked anxiously for Freddie, but he just nonchalantly poured Mel a cup of coffee. My heart slowed down as I sat quietly and listened. Mel never even looked my way.

The conversation turned to life on Main Street. It suddenly hit me—I was a fly on the wall of a crucial civic gathering. Each man had a Christmas assignment or two—groceries from Jensen's, clothing from Allingers, household goods from Thiel and Olsen, car repairs from Bear Lake Motor, haircuts from Grimes Barber Shop, building supplies from the lumber yard, and more. Of course, rolls, pies and turnovers from the Royal Bakery. The list of recipients was long, very long. Many were widows; others, families in need. As the group finalized delivery plans, Freddie came over to me.

"Your dad is already home."

"Ace, Ross will go with you. He can be your runner."

Ace Veeley had a severe limp and usually used a cane. We left the Royal Bakery, picked up the boxes at various locations, and began the deliveries. The fog had not yet lifted, but the town was very much alive. Mr. Veeley explained that sometimes they gave folks a little cash, but the ones on his list all had problems with alcohol, so no money—just food, nothing they could sell or drink.

"Don't ask any questions," he advised me. "Just make sure someone is home. There is no need to answer a question. Just tell them it is Christmas and their town appreciates them."

We drove half a block to "Rougie's" place behind Rich Motor. I hoped she did not recognize me because we often rang her doorbell and ran, or at times, cut through her front yard. She had bright red rouge circles on her cheeks and screamed at everyone. All day in the summer she sat in a chair on her porch holding her garden hose, squirting anyone who came near. Her empty chair sat on the porch as if waiting for spring to come. It took some real pounding to get her and her cat herd to the door. She said nothing and I muttered "Merry Christmas."

Next we turned back onto Main Street to Bear Lake Motor, and parked in front of Josie (and her son Kenny) Drivers' home. The stately wooden Victorian home was the only house downtown that was surrounded by stores. As with Rougie, Josie was a porch sitter. However, no one ever bothered her as she sat and observed everything happening on Main Street. Kenny always seemed to be drunk. Josie invited me in, but I said that we had to hurry. I took special notice of her long gray hair pulled up in a knot on the top of her head because I had always been curious about that funny hairdo.

She kindly invited me to "come and stay when we can visit."

"Thank you, Ma'am, I will. Merry Christmas." I did not see Kenny, which was good because Max and his friends teased him a lot and I did not want to be mistaken for my brother.

The last home was Stan Naylor's. Stan painted the signs on everyone's storefront, usually more often than needed. A magnificent talent, he only painted when drunk. To a young boy, Stan Naylor was just a joke, someone we laughed at or made fun of; sometimes we even moved his ladder. His home was a cluttered mess with no evidence of Christmas. His shapeless and paint-stained dress hat sat cocked to one side of his head as he looked me over at the door. It took me three trips to deliver the groceries and fruit to him, as well as a large box of painting supplies. He remained speechless as he strained to see who was in the pickup.

"Mr. Naylor, Merry Christmas from your friends."

His bony hand grabbed my shoulder; he looked me over and quietly said, "Christmas is good. Yes, Christmas is good."

When I got back in the truck, Mr. Veeley observed, "Freddie said to take you back to the bakery." I had almost forgotten about my time of reckoning. When we returned to the bakery, it was filled with people picking up their orders of signature Royal Bakery hard rolls and other baked goods. Not knowing what to do, I again sat miserably on the stool near the wall, reflecting on the morning's events. After a short while, Freddie walked over and said to me, "Go on home. Tell your folks how you spent the morning—A to Z."

"Everything?"

"That is what A to Z means—OK?"

"Yes sir. Thank you."

"Thanks for helping Ace."

I jogged back up Main Street, at Sixth Street turning north to cut through the junior high block and back to my home. When I arrived, everyone in the family was gone but Dad and my younger brothers, Reed and Brent. This was the third Christmas in our new home with central heat, running water, and indoor plumbing. I went into the bathroom, sat by the warm heat vent and thawed out while I developed a confessional plan.

"Rabbit" (one of Dad's many nicknames for me), Dad asked, "what were you doing at the Royal Bakery?"

That made it an easy transition and I blurted out the morning's events. However, I carefully avoided going into the summer's pop bottle-gathering escapades.

"Do you know how irritating a harmonica can be?" was his immediate response.

We talked briefly about how hard it was for people to get by and that if we deprived them of any possible income, we all suffered. That was all that was said about that saga—ever.

Later in the afternoon he bundled up the three of us and drove down Main Street, pointing out every business and telling us how many families were supported by each one. He then took some checks that Mother had written, and paid bills (in full) at the lumber yard, the grocery store, and the seed company. Dad's subtle way of reminding us that these were the people who took care of us all year.

Christmas is about community, loyalty, and support. It is about giving and forgiving—about respect and love. That Christmas of 1951, I learned that it really does take a community to raise a child. And for that, I remain forever grateful.

Raymond and Zora Peterson, 1935

Dad, Mom, baby Ross,
Max, Donna Lee
—trip to Reno, 1942

Clockwise from left: Donna Lee, Karl, Max, Ross 1944

Dad and Uncle Royal stand
atop horse

Ross stands in front of first
home on North Fourth Street,
Montpelier, 1947

Cousin Ron Larsen rides in
front of Ross, 1946

Pacific Fruit Express Company
where dad worked from 1940–1954

Snow–covered farm equipment

Courtesy of Ross & Linda Stephens Walker

Peterson family's haystacks had rounded tops and flat sides.

"Geese on Top of a Haystack" by John Lambing/Alamy Stock Photo, by permission

Dad listening to Friday night fights ca. 1949. Peterson family did not get television until late 1950s.

Dad at Christmas, 1953

Thiel and Olsen hardware store gun counter, 1950s

6

A Christmas for Dad

If the skies did not drop heavy snow at Christmastime in Bear Lake County, Idaho they cleared, and the thermometer dipped well below zero. Christmas Eve 1953 was clear and very cold. There had been plenty of snow earlier because the huge pile in the middle of Montpelier's Main Street had already reached twelve feet high, near where the first island of giant blue spruce trees stood between seventh and eighth streets. The snow banks along the roadsides created a bobsled-run effect and colorful Christmas lights illuminated both the large spruce trees as well as the Main Street shopping area.

It had been so cold the day after Thanksgiving that I had wanted to forego the long lines waiting to get a small brown paper bag of hardtack, frozen gumdrops, three chocolates, and peanuts from Santa. My younger brothers, Reed and Brent, made me stay until they got their candy. We got the same bag, different Santa, at church a couple of weeks later.

As Max and I milked the cows in Elton Bunn's barn early on Christmas Eve, we once again discussed our mother's Christmas wish. Just before we left the house, she had said, "Think of the Savior's gifts, not just His birth." She started "working us" in late November and subtlety was not her strong suit.

"Nineteen fifty-three is significant because it is the last year we will all be together as a family," she said.

"What do you mean?"

"Karl is leaving on his mission to New York, Donna Lee is away at college, and in two years a lot can happen."

"Well, we are here, and they might be, too," said Max.

Mother focused on us because 1953 had been an unusual year. As automatic heaters and freezers invaded the Pacific Fruit Express railway cars, Dad's job was in jeopardy. Although he had a dozen years at PFE, his work was seasonal and involved lighting charcoal heaters in some cars and icing others. Automation ultimately ended the PFE and Dad's job.

Our farming operation proved marginal in the best of times, but in 1953 we had put up a lot of hay for other people. Using our two teams of horses and the necessary equipment, we had worked hard. Max made $5 a day and I got $3 for driving the pull-up and cleaning up around the "ricker." Karl and Dad split the rest. Dad also gave Max and me the bull calves from the milk cows, which we sold in the fall. Once Dad and the owners of the hay measured the stacks to determine how many tons we had stacked, they settled and we were paid.

Then Dad went to the lumber yard, feed store, grocery store, and hardware store, and paid off bills. When winter came, he worked at the PFE and we received a steady paycheck. Our only other income was a small twice-monthly milk check.

By early November Max and I were flush. Together we had nearly $400 put away, and at ages fifteen and twelve, all we could think of were ball gloves and gym shoes. Mother had different ideas. She reminded us of tithing, which we paid, although I complained because I thought kids should be exempt. The Sunday following Thanksgiving she turned up the heat.

"Don't you think your Dad would look good in a suit?"

"In a suit? You mean a Sunday suit?"

"Yes," she said, her blue eyes sparkling.

There was no further discussion, but the seed had been planted. We could not imagine Dad in a suit. I could remember him at church only when we performed, but he was strictly back row material. Why waste money on a suit?

That night as we milked, I asked Max. "Why does she want a suit?"

"She wants him to go to church, I guess."

"He'd go if he wanted to, wouldn't he?"

"Maybe he'd feel better if he had a suit. I don't know." Then he chuckled, "He could put his velvet can in a side pocket." We both laughed as we pulled at the cows' teats.

Dad rolled his own cigarettes. He had it down to an art form. In a boyhood accident he had shot off two fingers and part of the thumb on his left hand; thus he would hold the paper in his right hand, pour the tobacco in with his bad hand, put away the tin, lick the paper, roll it together, put the finished product in his mouth, and reach down and strike a match on the dashboard. All of this while driving. Those smashed, soggy cigarettes emitted a memorable odor, lasted about four drags, and then Dad would deftly squeeze the end and flip it out the truck window.

The problem was that we had already decided on what we wanted to get Dad. One morning while delivering papers, Max thought out loud.

"We need to get Dad a new rifle. That old 30.06 is haywire and he has never had a new gun. We need the meat and he'd always be on target with a decent rifle." That made a lot of sense to me. Rifle, yes—suit, no.

The last Saturday before Christmas we started looking at rifles. We owned a lever-action 25.20, a single shot 22, and the 30.06. I liked the 25.20 because I shot left-handed and bolt actions were always on the right side. Every fall we hunted deer for food. Our goal was to get even with the deer that fed on our grain and alfalfa, but we also went into the mountains.

A new rifle for Dad seemed totally appropriate. We focused our attention on Thiel and Olsen's, a hardware store that actually had some of everything. Since neither of us had ever bought a gun, or much else for that matter, we relied on our Dad's friends who ran the stores. Al Thiel was a large, bald man who usually sat at a desk and let clerks handle the customers. For some reason, Max felt we needed to deal with one of the owners.

"Mr. Thiel, we would like to buy our Dad a rifle for Christmas," Max gathered as much bass in his voice as he could muster.

"Does Raymond know?"

"No, we want to surprise him."

"Do you know what he likes?"

"No, he just needs a new rifle."

Al Thiel probably knew a few things our Dad really needed, but we persisted. We looked at a number of shiny new rifles of various power and serious price differences. Mr. Thiel wandered back to his desk as we discussed the merits of each rifle. Our main concern was the price. Dad could hit anything with anything, but we decided to analyze our resources. As we left the store, we assured Mr. Thiel, "We'll be back."

"Let's buy everyone's gift," I suggested, "then see what is left over for the rifle." We started home through the piles of snow, but then decided on another approach.

"We have plenty of money, reasoned Max, "and if we go in together on everyone's presents, we can get them something nice."

Our first stop was E.L. Burgoyne's clothing store to get something for Karl to use on his mission. Mother had suggested white shirts or socks. We'd been told that he needed to dress like church every day and needed two suits and all kinds of other items.

"Hey, Max," I ventured, "since we're financing his love life now, let's just tear up his IOU's." Karl borrowed a little from us for every date, and as his dating was going to end for two years, he seemed to be accumulating many memories.

"No. He's into us for a lot more than a couple of white shirts."

"You know he'll never pay us back."

Max thought a long time before answering. "It would be dumb to open a present of some scraps of paper. Besides, the folks don't know he's been borrowing from us. I say two shirts, two pair of socks."

Elmer Burgoyne helped us select the right sizes and complimented us on our generosity. Then he added, "Your mother said you may want to look at some suits." Max quickly responded, "Not today, Mr. Burgoyne, but thanks." Mother had engaged a co-conspirator. No more shopping at Burgoyne's. We went to Allinger's and got one of the clerks to pick out a sweater for our sister, Donna Lee; then off to M. H. King's to get some toys for our younger brothers, Reed and Brent.

"Reed would be happy with a stick horse," said Max, "that's all he needs, just one red birch willow stick horse."

We found some toys. Reed and Brent were three years apart, but we always bought them the same thing or wrapped up one package and wrote, "To Reed and Brent." We never wrote nicknames on the label, or it would have read, "To Riches and Rone." They were seven and four, but Rone, the youngest, never realized they were not the same age.

We crossed Main Street to the Fair Store to look for something for Mother. As usual it was a kitchen item or an apron or some other memorable thing. The Fair Store, operated by Abie Thorpe, had pungent, oiled, dark wood floors and amazing glass-covered display cases, but we were in a hurry and didn't have time to linger. The temperature continued to drop and we needed to go do chores. All of our time was spent on the rifle and we had not yet made a decision. Christmas was on Tuesday. Only one more shopping day.

After we'd placed all of our new purchases under the tree, we took off for the barn. Dad was working swing shift, so we milked in the evening and he did chores in the morning. On Sunday he worked alone as we all went to church. By the time we got home, he was finished with all the feeding and milking. Dad drove a Dodge three-quarter-ton truck with a small cattle rack. He had sold our 1948 Kaiser and planned to use Karl's Studebaker while he was on his mission. So we usually walked.

Following church Mother said, "Where is the gift for your Dad?"

"Oh, it's a surprise," I answered.

Max added, "We'll just put it out like Santa does on Christmas Eve."

She had to know. "Did you go to Burgoyne's?"

"Yes."

"Did you get the suit?"

"Wait and see. He'll be really happy." Max hesitated to say more.

She stared at us. We squirmed.

Mother liked control, not surprises. "I am very proud of you for making this a special Christmas."

That night we tried to figure out what to do. Since Karl was home from college, I had moved into the north bedroom upstairs where Reed and Brent slept in one single bed, me in another. Karl and Max had the south bedroom. Karl always told us about every movie he'd seen while in Logan at Utah State Agricultural College (later Utah State University). He had every detail and it took as long for him to re-tell the story as it must have taken to watch the darn thing.

On Monday morning, Christmas Eve, we decided to tell Mother that we had purchased the rifle and that a suit would have to wait. At least she'd not be surprised the next morning. She did not take it well. Not at all. She shook her head from side to side and gave a little clucking sound that signified displeasure. Not a word.

Our enthusiastic request to take the food gifts to neighbors and friends was accepted, but her demeanor did not change. She was not sulking. A lot of her personal dreams had crashed on the rocks of everyday life. She knew how to lose and still dream. Her losses were temporary and short-lived.

We got some money and went back to Thiel and Olsen's. "Mr. Thiel, we have decided on the 300 Savage and we'd like a box of bullets to go with it." Standing tall and being positive sent a clear message. There was no argument. We tucked the shells into the box and paid $149 for the rifle. Mrs. Rasmussen and Mrs. Wilcox gift-wrapped it for us and we proudly walked home with our bounty. Dad deserved a rifle.

Without anyone watching, we quietly took it upstairs and put it under the bed before getting ready to go do chores. Then Mother played her ace. She held it for last because she thought we'd do as she wished.

"Do you know why we sold the Kaiser?'

"Well, we don't need that many cars," I said.

"It's older than Karl's car," Max added.

"We needed the money to get Karl ready, but we have payments to make and paychecks are not regular in the summer."

"We'd better go," Max said. He sensed the knockout blow.

"What happened to the Kaiser last fall?" she asked.

"Come on, Mother, that's history."

Max and I had wrecked the car. While Max plowed, Reed and I listened to the car radio and ran the battery down. So Max hooked the tractor onto the car and pulled me across the field, where I popped the clutch and proceeded to tear out the left side of the car on the plows behind the tractor. The putrid green car was ugly before the collision, but after, it was really ugly! The new paint did not match.

"We had to use Dad's summer money to fix the car so we could sell it."

Her words were soft, but firm.

"We would have paid for it," said Max.

But we had not volunteered.

She finally said, "Think of the Savior's gifts, not just what you might get or can give as presents."

We hurried to do the chores. Now in Bunn's barn on Christmas Eve, we finally capitulated. Rehashing our purchases, we decided to go right from milking to Burgoyne's Store. The stores closed at 6 p.m. We could pick up the milk cans later. As we ran toward town, Max wondered aloud whether we were showing up our siblings by buying so much.

At 5:55 p.m., accompanied by the stench of fresh milk and fresh manure, we trudged into Burgoyne's. Elmer and Sydney Burgoyne acted as if all the choices were ours. Mysteriously, they brought out a dark blue suit, Dad's exact size, and the pants were cuffed. They were sure this would really please our Dad. They also had dress shoes, socks, tie, shirt, and even a belt ready. After asking them to add a church book to the purchases, Max excused himself and said he would be right back.

I was really nervous because we had not gone home to get our money, so after Max's return, the Burgoynes let each of us sign a charge slip. The cost—about the same as the rifle. They gift-wrapped every item individually and we left for our house six blocks away. The clear, star-filled night was very cold; our money was spent, and we felt warm.

We knocked on the front door, gave all the packages to Reed and Brent, and went back to the barn for the milk. We laughed and joked as we pulled the sleigh, laden with milk, through the snow. Later that night, Max sneaked the wrapped rifle and stuck it behind the tree. Reed followed him down the stairs and quickly checked out Santa's deposits.

1953 was our last Christmas together—just us. I have no memory of any gift I received. However, I can still recall the glistening in my Dad's eyes as he opened all the gifts. I don't know if he liked one better than the other. Mother sat in her rocker and cried as he showed his pleasure and thanked everyone. Then she opened her last gift—the one Max had gone to get the night before. It was a new electric frying pan with the church book inside.

Later, as we surveyed the gifts, propped against Dad's treasures were the cards, in Max's handwriting:

> *TO THE GREATEST*
> *DAD IN THE WORLD*
> *FROM*
> *ALL OF US*

Ginger and Bud in
full harness

7

A Lesson Learned

Kimball, my colleague and friend, called to ask a question that I have wrestled with for nearly five decades. "How do you balance compassion with class standards when assigning grades?" He explained the dilemma of being flooded by excuses and alibis and poor performance as well as legitimate explanations. Every semester there are some familiar rationalizations and a few original, very creative crises that account for less than stellar academic outcomes.

Kimball patiently listened to my usual balanced, philosophical discussion of fairness, and a consistency process, but was not satisfied. Then I told him the following story:

The final period of the day on the Friday before Christmas, 1954, was nearing the end when an eighth grade English teacher at the Montpelier Junior High School passed back a writing assignment. Each student had been asked to write an original short story. They were handed back randomly, not by alphabet or by seating assignment; my name was called last.

"Mr. Peterson, please come to the front of the room."

Everyone was eager to go to the Christmas party upstairs where three classrooms had been converted into a low-ceiling gymnasium. I quickly walked to the front, not sure why he had singled me out. Maybe my story had impressed him and he wanted to compliment me.

"Class-sit down! Be quiet and listen! Mr. Peterson, do you know what plagiarism is?"

"No," I whispered.

"Everyone listen. Plagiarism is when you copy someone else's work and call it your own. That is what you have done, young man. Anyone who copies or cheats, fails. Do you understand? Bring me the original and I will let you write your own story for half of the credit."

Quietly I stammered, "That *is* my own story. I wrote it all."

"Don't make it worse by lying," he shouted. "All of those names, details, are not the work of a thirteen-year-old! Take your seat!" He quickly ripped the paper into shreds.

I could feel moisture in my eyes, but decided to remain standing in front of the class and muttered, "I did not cheat."

"Young man, you are making it worse."

Thirty-five other eighth graders sat stunned. Suddenly, two of my lifelong friends, Jerry Bissegger and Bob Wigington, came and stood by me. Bob called the teacher by name. "Sir, Ross did not cheat. He doesn't need to!"

"Take your seats! Class dismissed!"

No one moved. Jerry spoke quietly, "All the players and teams are his and his brother's." He had read my story and witnessed some of it unfold in the Peterson living room. The final bell ending the school day rang. Still no one left.

"Bob, go get the Principal." Jerry and I stood in silence.

When the Principal, J. L. Jaussi, entered the classroom, it was obvious that Bob had told him why he had been summoned. Mr. Jaussi said, "Everyone go upstairs to the party in the gym." I did not leave, so Jerry and Bob stayed with me. There was less than a festive mood in the room.

Mr. Jaussi, also our next-door neighbor, asked for an explanation. The teacher reviewed his assessment of the short story, my unwillingness "to admit to the errors of my ways," and the subsequent disruption of the class. I said nothing, so Jerry started to defend me, but Mr. Jaussi asked all of us to sit.

He spoke firmly, looking directly at the teacher. "A Peterson might raid a garden, ring door bells, do more tricks than treats, tease and make mischief, but they do not cheat."

The teacher responded, "That paper was typed perfectly, probably edited, and all of those names could not be made up!"

I spoke up, "Donna Lee, my sister, typed it at her work. We made up all of the names."

Mr. Jaussi, gave me a glance that signaled "Be quiet!" His eyes stayed focused on the teacher as he asked, "You accused him in front of the entire class?"

"I was sure that he cheated and I wanted the class to learn about plagiarism."

Mr. Jaussi shook his head and turned to us. "Boys, I think you should go home—NOW. No party for you three. It is Christmas and I do not want 150 children babbling about this incident. I will handle this. Have a nice Christmas and remember basketball practice starts the day after New Year's day."

We went into the hall, grabbed our coats, boots, and gloves and left the junior high building. Once we hit the steps, Jerry asked, "Are you and Max still playing that basketball game?"

"Not this year. He and Karen are going steady. With basketball practice, milking and Karen, he does not have time."

Bob quizzed, "What about the baseball diamonds? Where are they?"

"I still play on them a little." We had an eight-team baseball league. Max created different fields for each time and drew them to scale on pieces of poster board. We developed a statistical probability analysis that divided the field into singles, doubles, triples, home runs, walks, and every imaginable way to make an out. To play, we flipped a small piece of plastic, cut from the tong of a fork, and where the "ball" stopped determined the outcome of the play.

"Those games are what caused the trouble with my story," I thought out loud. "The players and games became so real to me. My whole story was about our championship basketball game last year."

Jerry, who had two younger brothers, suggested that maybe Reed and Brent (my younger siblings) could take over the game playing. I told him I might try that during the holidays, but those two were still pretty young. Bob chipped in, "Well, we won't miss much at that dance in the gym. The girls are all so tall!"

Then he added, "I wish Dick had been in our class, he would have done some serious swearing at that teacher." We heartily agreed. Dick Grunig had a temper, liked to fight, and feared no one in authority. The thought of Dick chastising a teacher made us laugh for the first time that afternoon.

We parted ways once we reached Fifth Street. Jerry went south, Bob north, and I stopped at my house. I went directly upstairs to my room and changed into my chore clothes.

My younger brothers were playing the basketball game in our bedroom. Lying on the bed, I watched and when Reed asked me if I wanted to play, I declined by reminding them that Max had a high school basketball game tonight and we had to milk before he left. I stared at the ceiling as memories overcame me.

For as long as I could remember, our family entertained itself with cards, board games, the radio, and creative original games. Before we moved into our new house in 1948, I vaguely remembered my older brothers, Karl and Max drawing, coloring and cutting out football players. They lined them up and used their hands to move the players and an almond (as the football) back and forth across the linoleum.

When we moved into our Fifth Street home with two second-floor bedrooms, Max and I shared the north room. Max turned his artistic efforts to basketball. Fascinated by a 1951 movie about the Harlem Globetrotters in which the athletes played themselves, he drew a team of African Americans called the "Harlem World

Chasers" and then matched them against some college All-Stars.

Max measured a court to scale on our hardwood floor and laid three Red Ryder or Hardy Boys books at each end. Then he placed two "dice shakers" from our board games against a vertical book positioned on top of the three books. Following a couple of seasons on the floor, Max talked Dad out of a piece of plywood.

After cutting the court to a perfect scale, he carefully painted red out-of-bounds lines, the foul lines and a jump circle at mid-court. Then he nailed two-foot-high 2x4s on the ends of the court. A thin plywood square backboard was attached to the 2x4 and a heavy wire circle was somehow embedded into the backboard. We then lifted the court onto a card table and sat on chairs instead of crawling around on the floor.

This elevation of the playing facility was necessitated by a matriarchal threat over the wear and tear on the knees of our Levis. However, the new court was so large that the game left the bedroom and moved to the living room.

One of the most intriguing aspects of our game was that it was based on respect and honesty. Calling fouls, goal tending, or other infractions depended on being fair. Max also wisely let me win enough to make the races tight and the interest high. Many of our friends came to watch us move back and forth announcing, moving players and keeping complete statistics. Sometimes there were ten or twelve spectators with Reed and Brent positioned at each end to retrieve errant basketballs (marbles).

The story I wrote for eighth grade English class summarized our final game from the previous season. I kept the box score and described the game in amazing detail. Any cognizant teacher should have questioned that story coming from an eighth grader's mind (and his sister, Donna Lee's typewriter at Dr. Reed Rich's office).

The crazy thing is that in the story I wanted to change the outcome so my team won, but the actual result could not be altered. Max and his team won in the short story, but it was not really fiction. Ironically, that game was the last we ever played on the board on a card table in the living room in front of an audience.

I heard the door slam as I returned to reality. From my position on the bed, I turned over to watch Reed and Brent play for a minute. Max yelled up the stairs, "Let's go!" I got up from the bed and went with him to milk. I told him about the accusation of cheating, the melee, and coming home both embarrassed and proud of my friends.

He just laughed. Not once did he say we should "let the air out of the teacher's tires or light a match to a paper grocery bag full of fresh manure on his front porch, or even unhook his battery cables." His words instead were, "Next time, misspell a couple of words, forget the ending, do something to keep the teacher thinking he is the smartest." Then he added, "Your mistake was having Donna Lee type it. She automatically edits. It is a disease and she is always right. Besides, a typed paper makes the other students look bad."

"No way!" I shouted. "I asked her to type it just as I wrote it—maybe it is her fault."

"No, it doesn't matter," he laughed. "Trust me. She will always make it better. Let's look it over."

"We can't. He tore it up!"

"That's BS!"

"Well," I responded, "Mr. Jaussi said he'll transfer me to another class."

I waited for the revenge plan to come forth, but it never came. Max nestled his head in the cow's flank, leaned in for warmth and said, "Never embarrass a person in front of others." Following a pause, he added, "Hurry! I have a game tonight!"

"Max, maybe we should play another season this winter. What do you think?"

"Naw—I think we should turn it over to the brothers. Those games have been good to us, but we need to move on. If the Montpelier Bears are ever going to get to the state tournament in real basketball, it is this year. Next year you'll be in high school and life is different. Your story ended right and it is time." He thought for a minute. "Let's give the court to the little brothers for Christmas. I'll draw them some new teams."

"Well, I guess you're right. It might be time."

Max changed the subject, "Why don't you ride to Nounan with me if I take Karen home after the game?"

"OK, Dad will milk in the morning. Are we driving Karl's car or the truck?"

"Depends on the weather. By the way, did you change the story so you could win the game?"

I did not like him questioning my integrity, but I answered "No Way."

We drove Karl's 1950 Studebaker while he was on his mission. Dad drove a three-quarter-ton Dodge with a cattle rack and his dog "Ring" in the back who thought the truck was his.

"Do you think Karen will mind?" I asked.

"No problem, I don't like driving home alone that late on bad roads."

That made no sense to me because I would be no help if we got stuck or had a problem, but he asked.

"Well, I'll go if you don't leave me in the car too long when you walk her to the house. I get worried and almost freeze, besides "Blot Man" (Dad) said to keep an eye on you."

He then squirted me in the back of the head with milk from the cow's far side teat and laughed, "You're a kid. No worries. Ring never lets us out of his sight." (The next summer, Max and Karen, the truck and Ring, went to the drive-in theater to see "Lady and the Tramp." Ring never left the truck, but howled and barked at the screen until they unhooked the speaker and drove away.)

Mr. Jaussi left me in the English class and a quiet, but tense truce existed the rest of the school year. I did not ask Donna Lee to type a paper again until I got to college. If I ever had a fear, it was to grow up. Being a kid is fun and sharing those times with my sister, brothers and friends created memories beyond compare. In later years, I realized that Max kept playing the games to satisfy me, but even then, none of my teams ever won the league championships.

The Christmas gift Max gave me in 1954 was a philosophy of teaching that never left. A teacher's purpose is to provide learning opportunities for students. It is not to intimidate, embarrass or ridicule.

In reality, through my years of teaching I have heard boatloads of excuses, many half-truths, and a few lies. Some students have cheated and privately in my office have faced the gentle wrath of disappointment and consequences. So I told Kimball that the teachings of Jesus coincide with Max's counsel: "Never embarrass a person in front of others."

Main Street in winter, 1950s

SAFE
TARGET
1/28/13
Max Peterson

8
Friends in Misdeed

Bob Wigington and I had been friends and neighbors since birth. The Wigingtons lived a half-block away from the Petersons. Our two large families shared friendship and several children of corresponding ages. Bob and I were in the same class in school and same ward—for twelve years—and had the same mentality. Later we even went to the same two-year LDS mission, the same week, on the same train.

My last practical joke on Bob was to lock him out of his own apartment in Akron, Ohio on a very hot and humid night when he and his missionary companion were sleeping on an upstairs balcony. (If they had worn pajamas, they may not have been quite so agitated!)

It was early afternoon, Christmas Eve 1956. There was a loud knock at our door and Bob Wigington came crashing in before anyone could get to the door. His ever-present smile, booming voice and infectious laughter filled our living room.

"Hey, what's going on? Grandma said you needed to see me?"

The summer before, following our high school freshman year, Bob's family had moved to Cokeville, Wyoming. He and his brother Lynn returned regularly to Montpelier during the summer to play softball with us, often visiting his grandmother who lived across the street from our home. We stayed close.

"Bob, we need to talk."

I grabbed my coat and we walked across the street. It was really blowing and the icy wind cut our faces.

"This reminds me of running home from school and also of coming home from basketball trips at 2 a.m.," I said.

"I really miss that," Bob replied, "but what's the deal?"

"Man, I am afraid we are going to get hammered on the 'misplaced cars' episode from last summer."

"You're kidding! I'd forgotten about that."

Then we laughed and slugged each other's shoulder.

"Bob, do you remember when your Grandpa Wilcox died?

"Sure, but what does that have to do with moving cars?"

"When I looked in his casket, he did not have his pipe and he wasn't wearing bib overalls," I recalled.

Bob laughed. "He was always on the porch smoking that pipe."

"Yeah, and he wore those big engineer bib overalls."

"What does this have to do with those cars?"

"Well, I think the police are claiming they were stolen, not just moved."

"Darn, they found them, didn't they? And we didn't damage them."

We sat down on the snow bank and watched the ice skaters on the rink behind his grandma's house.

"Bob, remember when we were skiing and sledding up by the dump and you broke your leg?"

"Do I ever! I still feel the pain."

I laughed. "Your Uncle Warren just propped you up in the back seat of the car and we made a few more runs, drank hot chocolate, and then he took you home."

"I guess if you live through every beach landing in the Pacific, a broken leg doesn't call for concern. Hey, get on with this BS about auto theft!"

"OK, but we've got to get our memories together."

We carefully went over what led us to "borrow" and hide our scout leaders' cars last August. In a way it was their fault—they upset us, and they left the keys in their cars.

In the spring, just before the last week of school, our project-oriented Scout Master arranged a job for our troop to clean and mow the town cemetery in preparation for Memorial Day. We washed all the bird crap from the headstones, clipped around the tombstones and crosses, and mowed and raked. For over a week we worked our tails off before and after school. Our last morning was the Thursday before Memorial Day. It was also the last day of school.

As we finished, we had a contest to see who could catch the most field mice. Pretty soon, we had about thirty mice in a big ten-gallon can. No one claims credit for the idea, but Bob and I took them to school early that morning when only the janitor was there and carefully distributed them in the teachers' desks. Then we went home, cleaned up, and kind of forgot about it.

My first class was freshman English from Louise Adams, the drama teacher. She knew acting! I had barely settled in when I heard a soul-piercing scream and looked up as she vaulted onto a chair. Hearing the scream, Principal Harold Phillips came running across the hall and into the room. (Mr. Phillips was also my neighbor and former scoutmaster who had taught us World War II marching songs.)

Mrs. Adams pointed to the desk drawer as she slumped into her chair. My eyes met those of our principal, his remained focused as he nodded his head, and we left for his office. Since the scene was repeated in about six other classrooms, Bob and I were officially kicked out of school for the remainder of the year—one day. Soon, the whole town knew about it.

During the summer Bob moved to Cokeville, Wyoming, I worked, and we never had scout meetings. Our troop was supposed to have received $100 for the cemetery cleanup, so when the scout troop met the last Tuesday of August, we grilled our new leaders, Lund Arnell and Doug Henrie.

"Hey, how come we never had any outings? What happened to the money? When are we going to do something?"

They shut us up and said that they had talked to the Bishop and we were not allowed to spend the money because of the mice caper.

"That's unfair," I said. "Bob's gone, and the other guys are OK. That really stinks!"

"Are you questioning us and the Bishop?" Mr. Arnell said.

"Yes, I am. That's not right!"

"Well, when you have improved your behavior, we will see about going to Lava Hot Springs," which had an Olympic-size pool. End of discussion.

The next week Bob was in town and I told him about the confrontation. He decided to go with me to the scout meeting to plead our case. We walked down the alley directly to the old church. Ordinarily we played "Kick the Can" or "Red Rover," but there was only a small group of us that day. A new blue Volkswagen was parked in front of the church right next to an oversized Buick, our Scout Masters' cars.

Temptation reigned supreme. The keys were in the VW and the Buick was left open with a stick shift. In ten seconds we hatched a plan. I drove the VW and the rest pushed Doug Henrie's Buick back down the alley. We rolled the Buick into an old lean-to shed next to Earl Stephens' barn, closed the doors, and then drove the VW around the corner.

Opportunity jumped up and grabbed us. There was a dug-out basement on the corner of Lincoln and Fifth Street. Someone had poured a foundation, but only on three sides. We carefully drove the VW up Rosie's Hill and down into the basement. Then we covered the car with a tarp and brush, carefully avoiding scratching it. We did not go back to the church.

The VW was found the next day and then we heard they were treating the second disappearance as a theft. After two days, I put an unsigned note, written left-handed, to Police Chief Sid Teuscher, giving him the location of the Buick. Sid had parked in front of the Jewell café having coffee and left the doors unlocked. I slipped the note inside Sid's car. The car owners had filed theft and damage charges, so the better part of wisdom called for us to lay low.

Bob and I chuckled as we went back through the story. Some of the best pranks are those that keep people in the dark.

"So what's the deal now?" Bob asked.

"Well, the Bishop came into priesthood meeting last week and said Doug and Lund were going to pressure the police to punish the culprits."

"They're bluffing!" Bob almost shouted.

"I think we damaged the VW a little," I said, "but I don't know why they can't forget it. I guess we're OK."

"Who knows about this?"

"My dad."

"How did he find out?"

"He always knows because we do what he used to do, and he just knows. Anyway, he knew I was upset over the money and the unfairness of the treatment of the other guys."

"So?" Bob asked.

"It's a quiet 'get-even' deal that runs in our veins."

Bob blurted out, "Why are they filing charges and pressing for punishment?"

"I think Dad talked to Sid and if we just go talk to him and quietly confess, he can close the book. You don't have other problems with the cops, do you?"

"No, not here. Cokeville's been a little crazy."

"Look, it's Christmas. I don't want this hanging over our heads. I'd rather tell Sid than the Bishop and then go through all that repentance stuff."

"Yeah, we might have to apologize to the whole ward."

We planned a brief non-detailed confessional—in the Christmas spirit. The problem was that Sid was an imposing figure and not a churchgoer. He was a former boxer with broad shoulders and a few bones that had been relocated around his face. His son Mike was our age and our friend. That should help.

We walked toward City Hall.

"Do we have to do this?" Bob asked. "What if he starts asking about other stuff?"

"We can't tell on Max and Dean or anyone else. This is about us and one misunderstood prank—not a crime."

Sid Teuscher was magnanimous and full of the Christmas spirit of charity and forgiveness. I think he had forgotten about the case even as he said, "It is on the unsolved list." Sid promised us there would be no charges "if you apologize to the two families." Then he asked a question I had not even considered, "Why them? They had not done anything to you." He was right, and any unlocked cars and their owners could have been our victims.

That was a low blow, but we had no choice. Everyone was trying to teach us lessons. A successful unsolved prank is a great lesson.

"Listen, Bob, you've moved, you're not charged, you helped me get this far. There is no need for you to go see them. I have to look at them every Sunday."

After Bob left, I walked alone to the two homes whose families we had embarrassed by moving their cars. Dad and the police chief were right. No one could scream at a repentant sinner on Christmas Eve. Apologizing becomes easier with practice and Dad and Sid convinced me that a police record at age fifteen was not wise.

Mother had asked me to deliver loaves of homemade bread to families, so I planned to use some of the bread for a peace offering, and prepared to appear chastened and humble. Reed and Brent helped me with most of the houses, but I did not want them to witness my confession.

When I left the house, Mother told me to hurry because my sister, Donna Lee, her husband Darrell, and new baby were coming home for Christmas. What a way to spend Christmas Eve!

The new wet snow was piling up deep on the road as I pulled a sleigh with a box full of bread. The irony is that I did not like to drive cars, only tractors or trucks. I trudged through the heavy new snow. Mother had sent three towels to cover the bread, but the towels became wet and the warmth was soon gone. The Henries were less than thrilled that it had taken me so long to admit the ill-advised prank, but said to "forget it" and they hoped I had learned my lesson.

I saved my visit to Lund Arnell until last, as the Volkswagen had been new and was more prized. His home had every light on and their three little children were running around everywhere. I could not see the parents, but I assumed they were at home because the snow on the driveway lay deep and undisturbed. I knocked loudly.

"Hi, are your parents at home?" I asked the three sets of eyes that opened the door a crack. No answer. "Please give them this bread and have a Merry Christmas." I handed them the bread and turned away as someone yelled from inside the house,

"Who is it? Come in! Can you help?"

I opened the door and Lund greeted me.

"Oh, it's you. My wife is in labor and she needs help."

"What can I do?"

"Nothing. I'll call the hospital and doctor. Just leave. Oh, please tell your mother to send someone to tend the babies."

I started to leave and realized that the little VW could not get out of the driveway, so I grabbed the snow shovel and started shoveling. The driveway was short, but there was a big snow ridge left by the snowplow where the driveway met the road. The garage door opened and the car backed out. I hurried. The snow kept coming and the VW looked tiny with little or no clearance. I shoveled like mad and broke through the snowplow's ridge.

Lund tried to back through the snow as fast as possible, but the snow bank stopped him. He drove forward and then with engine roaring, tried again and again. In between, I tried to scoop out more snow, but it was packing hard. Mrs. Arnell was moaning as he jumped out to shovel. Since the engine was in the back, when he hit the snow bank, the front end rose up. I jumped on the front and he blasted back again, and as he broke through he turned sharply, throwing me into the road. They sped off and suddenly I heard crying children. I wondered, "How do they put four children in a Volkswagen?"

Walking back to the house, I tried in vain to calm the children. All three were hysterical. I found the phone.

"Hey Reed, where's Mother?"

"Mom, can you help me? Here's the deal," and I explained my dilemma. In the meantime, the children were still screaming. I thought of candy, but one child was still a baby. Finally, I thought I could let them open a present. Unable to find any books or stories, I tried to remember the story of the birth of Jesus. The children were not comforted and neither was I.

Glancing at the tree, I spotted a little ornament, which was a baby in a manger, and then I found some miniature toy animals. When I laid down on the floor to put together a nativity, the children laid by me and watched. That calmed them down some, so I began to talk about homeless people having a baby in a stable and how a bunch of shepherds saw a star and herded all of the sheep in the valley toward the manger.

Thankfully, Mother came before I got to the Wise Men. I always struggled with "Gold, Frankincense and Myrrh," and then they told me in Seminary that Joseph and Mary had left the stable before they got there. Why not give the little boy some Lincoln Logs or Tinker Toys? He was the son of a carpenter. Mother sent me home to help get the house ready for our Christmas visitors.

The baby arrived after midnight and all went well. I never got to apologize nor did I really learn a lesson about pranks or teasing, but I did learn that Christmas has a way of helping us dig real deep and become better, even if for just one night. That makes it worth the pomp and circumstance and myths and unnecessary presents. For me, Christmas is about memories, not pageants or presents.

I walked home, dragging the empty sleigh, and when I saw the lights were on, went directly to Bob's grandmother's home.

She answered the door. "Is Bob here?"

"Come in." Grandma Wilcox gave me hot chocolate and we all visited.

"Well, I need to go spend some time with my family. Thanks."

Bob followed me out onto the porch. "How did it go?"

"It was good to get it over with. Arnells were having a baby on Christmas. That was unreal. I hate that Volkswagen! I hope Lund never leaves those stupid keys in it again."

"See you tomorrow."

"Thanks for hanging with me, Bob."

I think of my good friend Bob Wigington every Christmas. It has been many years since he died of heart and diabetes complications following a severe stroke. When his wife Karen asked me to speak at his funeral, it was an easy call. Of course, at a funeral I chose not to tell the best stories of our youth . . .

I miss my friend. Very much.

WINTER DRINK

Max Peterson

9
Jerry's Homecoming

"Jerry's coming home for Christmas!" Mike Brown shouted about his first cousin as he came into basketball practice. The Montpelier High School gymnasium was still fairly new in 1956, but the boys' dressing room reeked with the odor of steamy teenage sweat.

Mike's words erased any unpleasant smell, sight, or sound that day. They were a ray of light in a dismal fall. My friend Jerry Bissegger, a sophomore running back on our football team, had awakened one morning before practice in August and his legs simply could not move. Diagnosed with the feared polio, he was whisked to Pocatello, then to a rehabilitation facility in Boise, 350 miles from Montpelier.

Polio was one of the most feared communicable diseases in the world. At its peak in the 1950s, polio paralyzed or killed over a half-million people each year, wreaking havoc especially among children. In 1952 alone, nearly 60,000 American children were infected; 3,000 died and thousands were paralyzed.

Jerry's dad, a railroader, had died in a tragic car accident two years earlier; however, the Union Pacific still gave his survivors free passes, so Jerry came home by train. He had regained some mobility, but his muscles suffered permanent damage.

Later that night, I sat on my bed and withdrew into a brooding melancholy. There was no way to explain why Jerry, of all my friends, was the one who got that disease. Or why had my brother-in-law been the victim of a freak military accident in April in Europe that left him partially blind and with his brain damaged? Why had the Wigingtons moved to Wyoming?

With Jerry's polio and Lynn and Bob's moving, we didn't win a single football or basketball game that year. Nothing seemed fair. My brother Max had left for college and I had a lonely room to myself. Another older brother, Karl, got married; my sister Donna Lee, her new baby, and her husband Darrell lived with us after he was released from the hospital.

Life was turned upside down in Montpelier.

My nightly prayers seeking immediate, positive response, remained unanswered and I began to have doubts about my faith. I brooded through the night. I tried to think good thoughts. There had been many positively wonderful events in 1956, beginning with the birth of my first nephew. Then the Yankees won the World Series and Don Larsen pitched a perfect game. (My avid Yankee-fan dad was thrilled.) And in late October, I experienced a religious revelation.

Adjacent to our high school is an LDS (Mormon) Seminary building in which students may receive Christian religious instruction as part of their high school curriculum. During my freshman year of high school we had studied the Old Testament, a rather frightening experience for a fourteen-year-old. It seemed at times that God really had a bad attitude, lacked patience, and asked people to do peculiar things.

There was so much violence and the good, "chosen" guys often lost. The Abraham-Isaac sacrifice story seemed weird; Noah and the flood saw numerous innocent kids and many animals drown. Elijah and the bears eating children and Job's trials pushed me over the top. I sympathized with all the Egyptians who were wiped out because Pharaoh was a stubborn fool. The God of most of 1956 seemed like an Old Testament God.

As sophomores, we examined the New Testament, so enter—Jesus Christ. He fed the hungry, He healed the sick, He liked children, and most of all, He was into forgiveness. Jesus hung out with the common folk and went after the establishment and the wealthy. Gradually religion appeared more attractive to me. One October day the school held an assembly to hear Idaho's Frank Church, Democratic candidate for the US. Senate. He was young, tall, handsome, and a great orator.

A.M. Rich, our history teacher, introduced him and Church started talking about feeding the poor, helping the veterans, creating better schools, and providing better health care. That is when the revelation came to me as clearly as if I had heard a voice. "Jesus is a Democrat!" For a few days I was ecstatic. However, neither the Yankees beating the Dodgers, nor Frank Church winning, nor Jesus being a Democrat broke my December mood.

By Christmastime, fairness was still an issue and once I knew Jerry was coming home, my thoughts focused on him. I decided to go see him on Saturday evening after he had been home a couple of days. It was about a two-block walk to his home, and I sort of talked myself into stalling. One of the things Jerry and I enjoyed the most from first grade on was sledding on M Hill. So I took my old sleigh and walked up M Hill to think.

M Hill is a small hill directly east of Montpelier and south of the canyon through which US 89 winds its way to Wyoming. The hill has a large man-made M near its highest point, directly above Lincoln Street. According to local folklore, education officials Mr. Swenson and Mr. Winters surveyed it from an upper floor east window of the original Montpelier High School (which became the Junior High during our day).

The capital M was originally outlined by whitewashed rocks, then during the 1960s the community constructed a more permanent, solid-concrete letter, and installed electric lights. While we were in high school, prior to the new and improved M, we had two traditions relative to M Hill. One was to annually whitewash the rocks; the second (in conjunction with Homecoming) was to light fires in old rubber tires lying inside the rocks. The burning M was amazing!

To the south of the M was a great hill for sledding, with two main runs—"Face" and "Old Windy." Face was straight down the hill, across a ridge, over a canal and then down onto Washington (Main) Street. With a good run and jump onto the sleigh, we could almost make it to the stop sign where highways US 89 and US 30 intersect. If we were more adventuresome and patient, we chose a narrow road that began above the M and made a series of turns toward the bottom of the hill.

It was not that windy, but there were some turns and the one at the bottom was potentially dangerous. Rounding that last bend at top speed, we had to make a fast left turn over the bridge and then onto Main Street. The major dangers were from other sleds coming down Face, as well as the kids climbing back up the road. If everyone met at the bridge, someone would be hurt. At times, a few ended up in the frozen ditch. Others went sprawling as their legs were knocked out from under them. With no real supervision, chaos often prevailed.

Older boys built a snow jump at the bottom of Face, which caused us to take air and fly over the bridge. Many days after band practice Jerry and I had walked to his house, grabbed sleighs, and gone for a few rides. On Saturdays, all of our siblings joined us and the hill was covered with children pulling sleighs.

As the bodies were inevitably hammered, parents appeared, carrying their offspring home. There were many concussions, broken arms, and a few broken legs. Still, nothing felt more exciting than coming down that hill with snow in our faces and then making the split-second decision to go into the canal, roll off the sleigh, or just plow through everybody!

Sitting on my sleigh at the top of Face, my thoughts turned to Jerry. He loved football. His dad had been awarded the Whitman Trophy as the premier MHS football player in his senior year, and Jerry wanted to follow in his dad's footsteps. When World War II began, Jerry's dad, Rex, joined the military. As an infantryman, he fought in Europe and returned home a decorated veteran. Like many of Montpelier's young men, he got a job on the Union Pacific Railroad and began a career that provided a regular paycheck, security, and, for Montpelier, a great life.

In June 1954, at age 34, he was killed in a car accident, returning home from his work on a local train in Wyoming. As a youngster, I never knew what to say when faced with death, so I just tried to ignore it and say nothing. Jerry and his mother, Barbara, both quiet and soft-spoken, seemed to move on, along with his three younger siblings. The death of his dad motivated Jerry to succeed as a football player. When my friend did talk, he admitted that to be great at football had become an obsession.

Polio ended that dream.

As the snow accumulated, my mind drifted back to an incident in the eighth grade— explained in an earlier chapter. Our English teacher, in his first year, accused me of plagiarism in front of the entire class. Jerry rose, speaking with passion, and along with Bob Wigington, defended me in front of the class. I had written a short story based on a table-top basketball game my brother Max had invented and which we played almost every night. Jerry and Bob and many others had watched us play. My short story described a championship series between two fictitious teams. Jerry's courage and loyalty strengthened our friendship.

I glanced down on the lights of the city and then back to the M on the hill. M Hill was about to change. Someone had talked about building houses and the city wanted to restrict its use as a sledding hill. The thought brought me back to the present and I knew it was time to go see Jerry. I got a good run and came straight down the face. New snow blinded me as I shot over the bridge and followed tire tracks all the way to the Jewell café.

Crossing the highways to Jerry's house, the view down Main Street was amazing. U.S. Highways 89 and 30 shared four blocks of Main Street and then US 30 went south at Fourth Street toward Wyoming and US 89 went north for two blocks and then east toward Star Valley, Wyoming. Each of those four blocks on Main had islands down the center with four or five giant blue spruce trees. Covered with multi-colored lights and snow, the majestic trees brought Christmas to our town.

When I knocked on the Bisseggers' front door, it opened almost instantly. Many of our friends were there. I took off my overshoes and walked toward Jerry. He was sitting in a chair with a quilt covering most of his body. He looked frail, tired, and thin, but smiled as I walked toward him.

Jerry controlled the conversation. "Not one win in football?"

"No, but I played JV. You can't blame *me*."

"No blame. What else is new?"

"Basketball is the same—new coach, no plan, and little size. We are winning some JV games."

The small talk continued and others took their turn, one on one, with him. I was relieved I did not have to push a conversation, awkward, strained, and superficial. But even the smallest questions seemed too obviously painful.

"How do you feel? What do you do during rehabilitation? Are your therapists good? Do you feel you are making progress?" None of these questions were asked. With everyone jabbering and trying to be funny, I drifted into observer status.

Suddenly, Jerry looked at me and asked, "Where were you before you came here?"

"I went up to M Hill."

Someone questioned, "Why M Hill? That's for kids."

Jerry asked me directly, "What were you doing?"

"I just wanted to look over the town, try to figure some things out, and make one last run."

Jerry got a little misty and softly said, "Those were fun times."

Another person jumped in and talked about new houses on the hill and the end of sledding. But, Jerry interrupted, "Well?" he asked. "Did you figure anything out?"

"No, not really," I shook my head. "It just seems like Christmas is not the same."

His mother came in and quietly said Jerry needed to rest. She ushered us toward the door. I took my time putting my boots on and played with Jerry's younger brother Kevin and little sister Jan. Jerry called for me to come back beside him. Softly, almost whispering, he said "No more ball for me. I can play the trumpet and will get better. I hope they let me stay home. Don't worry."

Blinking back tears, I could only shake my head, slowly pull on my mittens, and wave. "I'll be back."

As I left Jerry's home and promised to see him often, his mother walked out with me and quietly thanked me for coming. She was so gentle and kind and comforting, but my thoughts were about *her* pain. It all seemed so fundamentally unfair. With the snow coming down a little harder, I pulled my sled toward Fourth Street.

As I crossed Main, the colored Christmas lights on the gigantic trees glowed softly through the snow. It looked like Christmas, but it just did not seem much like Christmas. I began to jog along the sidewalk, and then stopped abruptly, feeling guilty that I could run. As I passed Hooker's tiny market, I checked my pocket for loose change. Finding none, I walked faster.

At the corner of Lincoln and Fourth I saw A.M. Rich, our high school history teacher, shoveling the deep, wet snow from his porch and sidewalks. I stopped and asked if I could help. Mr. Rich taught only juniors and seniors, so I had not yet been in his classes, but my brothers and sister had enjoyed them. I did not want to talk about what was bothering me, but Mr. Rich offered an opening.

"Where have you been?" he asked.

"I went to see Jerry Bissegger. He came home from that rehab place in Boise."

"How is he doing?"

"He's got braces and crutches and I guess that's the way it will be."

"I thought he needed water exercise to regain the use of his legs. There are no pools here," ventured Mr. Rich.

"Mr. Rich, what do you think about fairness? This thing with Jerry—the polio, his dad getting killed. It's so unfair."

He stopped shoveling, leaned on the shovel and said nothing. I knew I could trust him; after all, he had married my mother's cousin and was a Democrat! That was good enough for any fifteen-year-old who had had a revelation.

"Just add in Donna Lee, my sister. She is 21, married, with a new baby, and her husband nearly got blown up in Germany. He's disabled at age 22." Bringing up my sister, who was one of his favorite students, only added to the silence.

Quietly I asked, "How can Heavenly Father just let bad things happen?"

Finally he spoke. "Don't blame God. Life is random. Do you know what I mean—random?"

"Does that mean we have no control?"

"No, there are a lot of things we do control, but accidents, diseases you cannot worry about. We try to prevent them and protect each other, but they happen. It may not be fair."

I then ventured into difficult territory to seek an answer. "If God knows and cares, why does it happen?"

"It's Christmas, but let's keep God out of this, OK?" Mr. Rich had been in the Army Air Corp in Europe during World War II and filled his quota of bombing missions. He knew "random" better than most. I never heard him talk about the war, but I think he knew every person whose name was etched in the county memorial marker. The heavy snow replaced what we had already shoveled, but when I started to shovel again, he stopped me.

Looking me directly in the eye, Mr. Rich said, "I was wrong to take God out of this. It is Christmas, and Jerry will get better and have a good life. It will be different and difficult, but he will do well." Mr. Rich took a deep breath and asked, "Have you ever talked to your parents about this?"

"No, sir. I'm just trying to sort it out and can't."

"Here is how I try to fight my way through it," he said. "Focus on how you treat others. If you want a religious answer, just read those "red words" in your Seminary Bible. Start with the Sermon on the Mount and end there. The way I read Jesus is that we can only do what we can do—feed the poor, take care of the sick, and help those who suffer; forgive the sinner, seek forgiveness, and do not throw stones at others."

I waited for more. I needed more. I could not find clarity.

"That's all! Thanks, let's shovel it one more time."

We went to work and I waited for more words. There was only silence. Often, great teachers do not need to speak. Mr. Rich thanked me again and I thanked him, found the rope to the sled and started toward home.

"Hey, Ross!" I turned, and Mr. Rich continued. "Life is not always fair. Celebrate Jesus' birth and live his words. That's all you can do. Begin with your family and friends. Follow the example of your parents." Once again I grabbed the rope to the sled and ran home.

"Mom, I'm home. Can we take the food baskets to people now?"

"That would be great! Here is the list." She didn't even act shocked that I had volunteered. Reed and Brent got bundled up and we loaded two sleighs. I ran upstairs to find an old shoebox and asked Mother to wrap it up for me. Our last stop was back at Bisseggers! Jerry's brother John let us in and I walked over to Jerry, handing him the box. He looked at me expectantly.

"Go ahead, you can open it now."

Jerry pulled the ribbon off and slowly removed the wrapping paper. When he opened the box, he started laughing. His mother and family members looked into the box, not imagining why we laughed. Inside were the paper basketball players Max had drawn, each of the six teams stacked according to height. I had never looked at them since the accusation of plagiarism.

"I don't understand—why this, why now?" Jerry muttered.

"I never thanked you. My dad says it is the little things that add up. Thanks for then and now!" We said our good-byes.

Reed, Brent, and I pelted every road sign, streetlight, and each other with snowballs all the way home.

We live life in the long run and things balance out, so fairness is a little random. Jerry became team manager for both football and basketball and always played the trumpet in the high school band. In one of the most interesting ironies, Jerry, Bob, Dean Swenson, and I—who started first grade together and graduated from high school together—all went to the same LDS mission the same week in October 1960, four years after my revelation. At the end of their missions two years later, on the day that I took Jerry Bissegger and Bob Wigington to board the train in Ft. Wayne, Indiana for their return to Montpelier, Jerry walked on without crutches or braces.

Mr. Rich left Montpelier in 1960, obtained a PhD, and has lived in Oregon ever since. After graduating from college, Jerry, with his wife Diane and their family, lived and worked in California. He did well—very well. As Jerry neared retirement, post polio syndrome gradually took away the use of his legs. He passed away in 2019 in Temecula, California.

Ross poses triumphant in front
of new home on
Fifth Street, 1948

Montpelier LDS
Third Ward

Mother writing letters to Donna Lee and Karl, 1955

Ross with prize-
winning 4-H calf,
1954

Charles M. "Tiny" Grant
Coach

Ross and new
Chevrolet, 1956

Montpelier High School

Harold Phillips
Scoutmaster and Principal

A.M. Rich
History Teacher

Lewis Munk
English Teacher

Louise Adams
English Teacher

Rich Theatre, 1956

E. L. Burgoyne and Sons clothing store

Aerial view of M Hill
Courtesy Ross Walker

One of the Peterson draft horses
ready for work

10
A Room at the Inn

"Amen" had barely slipped out of my friend Dick Aland's mouth when I burst from the Sunday School classroom, ran out the main door of the church, and raced for home. Beckoning was dinner of roast beef, potatoes and gravy, corn or peas, and a fruit turnover (made always with home-canned fruit). A Sunday ritual at the Peterson home in 1957.

Television and the National Football League entered our valley that fall as well; not at our house, but at the homes of a couple of friends. The TV sets required 50-foot antennas and the ensuing reception filled the screens with intermittent snow showers—at least it looked that way.

As soon as I finished my dinner, I grabbed my plate and utensils and put them in the sink.

Before anyone asked, I announced, "I'm going down to Becks' to watch the football game."

My dad responded, "Slow down. We need to talk." For a brief second I thought he might tell us we were going to get a television set for Christmas. My brothers and I had begged for one in October when the Braves played the Yankees in seven games, and won the World Series.

All of the games were day games. I had been excused from school to "do farm work," but actually ended up driving the tractor to either Becks' or Buscos' to watch the games. Dad found me out and I had to make it up on Saturdays, but it was worth it because my beloved Braves won the Series!

Since the arrival of winter, Dad's construction work had slowed and because the farm had not had a great year, a television was out of the question. I sat back down, but left my coat on. Dad turned to Mother and said, "Zora, tell them what we have decided."

I looked at Reed (11) and Brent (8) and then at my parents. We sat around the wooden dining room table, which at times, doubled as a Ping-Pong table and hosted numerous other board and card games. This meeting could not be good. In our family, things just happened. Meetings and discussions where the children were included were rare.

My mind raced through a number of possibilities. Are we moving? We had that discussion a few years earlier when the Pacific Fruit Express pulled out of Montpelier and with Dad's seniority, he could move to Blythe or El Centro, California. Mom and Dad decided to leave the Union Pacific and scratch out an existence in Idaho. In the past two years, my three older siblings had all married and were somewhere in college. Max had actually just been married two days earlier—maybe they got lost or snowbound or something? Perhaps it was some big announcement about Christmas. Like no gifts!

Mother's voice ended my meditation. "We have a problem in the ward." (Mother was the Relief Society president, so that usually meant chopping kindling, taking out garbage or shoveling walks. No big deal, and we collectively relaxed.) She continued, "There are four single women, all school teachers, living in that house behind the Adams' home." The long pause destroyed my relaxation.

"The house is too small and they are having some problems (another pause). So we have invited one of them to move in with us!"

"Which one?" I blurted out. Three of them were at the high school and one taught me in two classes. Suddenly I had a stake in the discussion.

"Miss Meiners. She will move in after Christmas break. She can stay in Donna Lee's room, next to the bathroom."

Reed should have yelled, "Foul!" He loved that heat vent in the bathroom right above the furnace. Every night he would cuddle with a blanket in front of the vent, getting everything warm, and then race upstairs and leap in bed. His reign near the heat vent was soon to be over.

If Brent had any idea that Miss Meiners was going to be the first of a decade of boarders, he should have screamed "No!" Instead, silence surrounded us and the thought of ridicule from my classmates engulfed me as I stared at the floor.

"You will all have to be kind. She is going to be here until June."

Finally I looked up and blurted out, "Why her?"

"She seems to have the most problems," Mother softly answered, "and the others are just tired of her crying all night."

"Mom, I have her in two classes and she cries all day. She is unhappy and the students show her no respect. The English classes are chaotic! Besides, I heard she has decided to quit."

"Ross, you need to be an example and be very nice and help her. She is going to finish out the year."

I looked pleadingly at Dad. He gave me a shrug.

"OK, but I'm going to have Mr. Phillips put me in different classes. This is not good! Do you have any idea what the other kids will say?"

That question received a horizontal head shake from Mother and a harsh glare from Dad. Reed then smarted off about my not having to go very far to "brown nose," so I just shook my head and left.

It was four blocks to the Downing Apartments where Bruce Beck and his mother June lived. Bruce had received an LDS mission call to Samoa and was just waiting to go in February. The friends his age were all away at college, so all fall he invited some of us younger guys to his house to watch games each Sunday. At least that is what we told our parents. Actually, we played Pinochle every Sunday afternoon between dinner and evening church. (Mother began to worry about what we were doing, so she had actually sent Max to spy on us earlier that fall.)

The TV was turned to the NFL game, but four of us were playing cards—not for money, but for intense, competitive fun. Every week Mrs. Beck set out sodas and nuts, or crackers or candy and it became an enjoyable ritual. Pinochle is a great mental game. You learn to "count cards." Max's report was honest in that he admitted we played cards, but he embellished the setting to include "dim lights, visors with green clear plastic brims, and stacks of poker chips."

At our home, we played Rook, which was quite similar to Pinochle, but not as difficult. The problem was face cards, which had become taboo in certain religious circles. I assured my parents there was no money exchanged. To say the least, it was light sin.

By the time I ran to the Becks' my friends had become impatient. The San Francisco 49'ers were ahead of the Detroit Lions 27-7. The game seemed finished, so the cards and the sharks were waiting. Everyone sensed I was distracted, but my partner that day, Ralph Shreve (Lassiter) never made a mistake and we normally read each other's moves perfectly.

As the Lions came back to win the game (31-27), and the clock moved toward the time for evening church, I called an end to the Pinochle. Bruce, Larry Grimes and Ralph looked surprised, but agreed. Finally I told them about Miss Meiners moving into our home after Christmas.

All of them bemoaned my fate of having a teacher move in with us, but especially one who had little respect and was subjected to endless teenage ridicule. "Look," I said, "I am sorry, but this has been a tough week and now Christmas is ruined because of the thought of Miss Meiners. And I'm just getting used to Max being gone."

"He's been in college for a year and a half," Ralph offered.

"Yes, but his stuff is still in our room, plus he came home every weekend, and all of last summer." I shook my head. "Now he is long gone." Then I recapped the past few days.

Max and Karen's reception had been held the night before and that was the night of the MHS girl's-choice Preference Ball. Since my presence at the reception was required, I turned down invitations to the dance and then the officers of the Pep Club informed me I had to be at the floorshow in case I was voted "Preferred Man." A guy without a date was definitely not preferred, but I wandered from the reception (being held at the Seminary building) over to the gym at 9:30 just in time to see Brent Price get crowned.

"It is weird that I could not even watch them get married because I was too young to attend the temple ceremony. Karl, Donna Lee and now Max—all married in the Temple and you can't prove it by me," I lamented.

Bruce just laughed and said, "This is not even a problem." Then his mother, who had been teaching Ralph how to iron his shirts, served us some pie before we left. She also offered some advice. "Christmas is not about us. It's about Jesus and his birth." Bruce chimed in by adding, "I have been studying a lot lately and I believe Jesus taught us that we sacrifice for each other and in some cases, for those we do not even know."

"For me, some trauma always hits me right about Christmastime," I replied. "There just seems to be a lot of problems and then we act like everyone is doing fine!"

Bruce's parents had divorced three years earlier, and June and Bruce moved from Pocatello back to Montpelier into a small apartment so he could be around friends and family. Ralph never said much, but it seemed his stepfather always treated him as an outsider. Both Bruce and Ralph knew troubles and sacrifice and looked to others for support.

Mrs. Beck spoke an economic reality. "Look, your parents may need a little money. Honestly, it will be easier on me to have Bruce in Samoa for two-and-a-half years than to have him in college. I am just happy you could all come here and show friendship. It has been good for us."

Larry, a barber's son, chimed in, "My dad told me that if my mom did not have her job at the Forest Service, we'd be in the poor house. A haircut is the easiest thing in the world to postpone."

The opportunity to listen soothed my attitude. There are times when my concern for self outweighs what is really important. My parents taught us that, without ever preaching, cajoling or forcing. My concern over what others would think if my teacher moved into our home subsided. I still did not like the loss of space and privacy, but chose to go home and tell my parents I could handle it. This did not even resemble the Christmas story. We had to think about real life.

Then when Ralph quietly said, "There are many nights I wish I had my own bed," my selfishness struck home.

As we broke up to go to three different Sacrament meetings, I suddenly realized that it was December 22! For most of my life I had usually ignored my Mother's birthday, just three days before Christmas. That day just simply got swallowed up by Christmas. With new awareness, I asked Bruce if he would drive me to the drugstore to get a card and something else for Mom. Unfortunately, it being Sunday, all three drugstores—Lowe's, Burgoyne's and Modern—were closed, as were the grocery stores.

We returned to the Beck's home and June Beck kindly gave me a beautiful handkerchief and a couple of empty cards with envelopes. I barely got home in time to change clothes and race to the church to take my place behind the Sacrament table. One of my friends, Calvin Burgoyne, was waiting for me to join him in blessing the sacrament.

After we finished and the congregation had been served, we stayed behind the table during the Christmas program. (As I sat there, I wished I could hear Reed's renditions of "I'm

Gettin' Nuttin' for Christmas" and "All I want for Christmas is my Two Front Teeth," but sadly, they weren't deemed appropriate for Sacrament meeting. Those songs always "stole the show" at the Ward Christmas Party! This was in part due to the fact that most of the congregation felt that Reed *should* get 'nuttin.')

I looked out over the congregation and noticed Miss Meiners sitting alone in the back corner of the chapel. The other three teachers sat together on the other side. As the program developed, I looked at the note cards and then slowly printed a message to my mother on one card. I folded the handkerchief and put it and the card in the envelope. I wrote Mom on the outside and handed it to her after church. On the second card I carefully wrote a note to my English teacher, Miss Meiners. As I passed Mr. Phillips on my way out, he said,

"Your mother said you wanted to talk to me."

"No, sir," I responded. "I think I have worked it out."

"You will be fine, but come and see me anytime."

By the time I made my way to the back of the chapel, Miss Meiners was gone. I ran out of the church and saw her walking alone. Catching up to her, I handed her the envelope and wished her a Merry Christmas.

Do I remember what I wrote on the two cards? To Miss Meiners, I penned, "I have no problem with you staying with us. I will be quiet in class and hope you learn to love teaching. Don't stay in the bathroom very long." On my Mother's 46th birthday, my note to her said simply, "OK, you win. Have a nice Birthday and thanks for teaching us to care. No promises. I will do my best. Happy Birthday and Merry Christmas, 1957—Love, Ross."

That Christmas has many footnotes. Miss Meiners left Montpelier in June, worked as a secretary and later married. She never taught type and Junior English again. Mother kept in touch with her. Then in late March my friend, Jeff Nye, told me that his mother had decided to move her family from Montpelier back to Ogden. I asked my parents if Jeff could stay with us until school was out. Of course they said "Yes."

With somewhat of an ulterior motive, I literally begged him to stay through my senior year. (Jeff, a freshman, was an exceptionally talented basketball player, and together with other gifted and tall freshmen, Delano Lyons, Russ Stuart, and Charlie Skinner, our team could be very good.) No deal. His mom needed him. And then the Skinners moved to Arizona. My hope for a great team diminished through another dose of reality.

Some years later Ralph, after a six-month stint in the Army Reserves, a mission to Raratonga, and battle with tuberculosis, showed up at my parent's home in the middle of the night. He stayed nine months, and had his own bed. (When Ralph left the Reserves, he went to college at USU and I helped him support himself by "counting cards" at various fraternities and apartments. Money was involved and by all accounts we succeeded admirably.)

Bruce returned from Samoa just as Larry and I left for missions in the Netherlands and Great Lakes, respectively. Bruce married, and he and Janet became our wonderful lifelong friends. I later married Larry's sister, Mary Kay, and the bond strengthened.

Neither the NFL nor Pinochle corrupted us, and our friendship transcended the years. When surrounded by memories of Christmas and personal sacrifice, friends and families sustain us as we attempt to follow the admonition of Jesus—

"AS I HAVE LOVED YOU,
LOVE ONE ANOTHER."

Ross and his father Raymond flank a baseball team they
coached. Their brother and son, Brent, is sitting
on the middle row, third from the right.

Christmas Cantata directed by Julliard alumnus
Wes Baker, 1958

11
"CHRISTMAS CANTATA"

Each year as the Christmas holidays approach, I am certain I will hear selections from Handel's "Messiah" and most assuredly the "Hallelujah Chorus" from the grand oratorio. When the chorus reaches the crescendo at the conclusion, I usually begin to laugh. The jocularity is not loud, nor boisterous, but a silent chuckling that begins deep in my stomach and bounces its way up my torso until the laughter bursts through my clenched teeth. The sacred musical classic deserves better, much better, but invariably my chuckle evolves into mirthquakes of laughter. The cause is memory—selected memory—and the memory creates the reaction.

Montpelier High School's annual Christmas Cantata represented the singular Christmas tradition at the school and in the community. The date of the holiday performance was generally the last day of class (or weekend) before Christmas break and nothing else in town or at school ever competed. Wesley R. Baker, the school's choral and band director, dictated the time and scheduled everything early. From October until the performance, the choir rehearsed the numbers and prepared for a performance of excellence.

In many respects Mr. Baker was the icon of culture in the community. Beyond his band and choral commitments, he gave private voice, piano, and band-instrument lessons before and after school. Some students used their study hall time for lessons.

Saturdays were also scheduled, whether for the Cantata, the spring concerts, or the competitive district music festivals; Mr. Baker demanded and usually received perfection from his students. He hand-picked the accompanists and soloists, and created trios, duets, and quartets to perform them.

More than any other event, though, the Christmas Cantata ruled. Every December, shimmering pale-blue choir robes appeared, the auditorium was magically transformed with impressive and stunning decorations, and a night of elegance came to Montpelier. Former MHS students, home from college, always came back to hear the Cantata while reliving each one's own past participation.

A graduate of Julliard in New York City, Wesley Baker landed in Montpelier as a result of the Great Depression. The Salt Lake City native and his new bride, Adele, a lovely Catholic lady from the east, came during the 1930s to the small Mormon, railroad and farming town because there were very few job offers and school superintendent A. J. Winters offered him one of the few.

Wes Baker was the "Music Man" without being a shyster. A high percentage of Montpelier school children played in the grade school, junior high, or high school bands. Adding the choral groups to his total of music students, most of Montpelier fell under the spell of his baton.

Parents bought into his program and although he was always demanding, sometimes critical, and even caustic, we stayed with him. He was quite original in his assessments of some recalcitrant kids, calling them, among other things, "just pieces of meat!"

At such moments of displeasure, his face turned purple all the way to the crown of his balding head. He scared us into submission and, despite ourselves, excellence.

The choir consisted of anyone older than a freshman who wanted to sing and could fit the class into their schedule. There were no formal tryouts, so each year Mr. Baker trained a choir of willing, yet mostly less-talented subjects. To be sure, those who had talent rose to the top and were chosen as soloists for the prime, traditional numbers. In Montpelier, the most coveted male solo was undoubtedly "Ave Maria." The mere singing of the number caused some concern among more narrow-minded Latter-day Saints (unless their son was chosen).

Someone else sang "The Rosary," causing the town gossips to whisper that he only chose those songs to please Mrs. Baker's cultural and religious roots.

After a time, people stopped complaining and took pleasure in the beauty of the traditional classical music, having gained an appreciation for something well out of their realm of experience. With time we just acknowledged and admired Mr. Baker's choices—always ending with the "Hallelujah Chorus."

For many years I attended the Cantata as a spectator and enjoyed the festive occasion. In our town most people supported every community endeavor. I played for years in Mr. Baker's band, but my senior year, by the mere whim of a dare, I asked Mr. Baker if I could join the choir.

School had been in session for a couple of weeks and I had a study hall the same time as chorus. Two weeks of boredom and mischief landed me in Principal Harold Phillips' office. He lectured me about being an example as student body president and reminded me of numerous earlier academic transgressions as well as the exacting standards of our new coach, Charles "Tiny" Grant. Coach Grant, a mountain of a man, introduced 'Ma'am" and "Sir" to our vocabulary as well as more wins in football and basketball than we had had in the previous three years combined.

"Mr. Phillips, there is not another class the hour of study hall," I explained.

He looked over the schedule and asked, "Have you thought about choir?"

"No, Sir, and I won't. Mr. Baker has standards."

"You used to sing in Scouts," he responded, laughing. He had been my Scoutmaster and taught us some World War II marching songs that we sang with considerable gusto. When we started marching around singing at a Court of Honor, "I've got a gal in every port, suing me for non-support, honey, oh baby mine," the Bishop released him and the fun was gone.

It saddened us because between seventh and eighth grade, he took us on the trip of a lifetime. We rode in the bed of his Ford pickup all the way from Montpelier to Utah's national parks, the Grand Canyon, Lake Meade and back.

Mr. Phillips then quietly said, "You can sing and I dare you to do it."

"That was before my voice changed."

He chuckled, then noticing Wes Baker in the hallway, went to the door and called him in. "Mr. Baker, Ross wants to ask you a question."

I had known Wesley R. Baker since the fourth grade and had never asked him a question. My sole purpose in band was to go unnoticed and I had failed.

"Yes, Mr. Peterson, how can I help you?"

"Mr. Phillips wants me in the choir," I said.

"That was not a question." He looked hard at me over the top of his glasses.

"Sir, may I join the chorus for this year?"

"What? Why? Have you ever sung? Your brothers never sang, but your sister did. She could do everything . . . What brought this about?"

"Well, Sir,—I lied, sort of—I always wanted to be part of the Cantata."

Mr. Phillips was enjoying this exchange, but fearing my next words, said, "He badly needs another class!"

Wesley R. Baker studied me and then acknowledged a truth. "The boys in your class might be the least-talented collection of vocalists ever assembled at this school. The juniors are going to save the choir, but I really do not need it to go from bad to worse." Then he really scared me.

"Sing the scale—start at C."

I looked helplessly toward Mr. Phillips, but he had turned his back. "If I do it here, does it mean I do not have to do it in front of the rest of the chorus?"

I remembered the first day of band each year when Mr. Baker had us play up and down the scales, alone. I could play the scales perfectly on the cornet at home or if Mr. Baker was in another county or another building. But the second he glared at me, my lips trembled and the sound that came from the trumpet would have scared any four-legged animal.

He sang a note and I softly followed him up the scale and down. Taking a deep breath, he shook his head.

"Mr. Baker, our class was the only one in the history of the Washington School that didn't participate in Hazel Jacobsen's annual operetta. She said we were 'not worth the effort.' (This may have been determined by her trying to control a class of twenty-six boys and eight girls.) My mother forced me into trying out, but not one member of our class was chosen."

Mr. Baker relented. "OK, you are in, but it is only because you need a class. Don't sing loud!"

Three months later, we were having our last rehearsal before the performance. We sang in our sky-blue robes and everyone looked angelic. I knew enough from band that the choir had some really weak sections and that the final number—the "Hallelujah Chorus"—

sounded terrible when the men sang. After the rehearsal, Mr. Baker asked if I would "Please stay a moment." He actually said "please" which made me suspicious.

I was headed for basketball practice and wanted to get going, but he called me into one of the little practice rooms off the stage and gave me three pieces of music. (I suddenly flashed back to when he called me in during seventh grade and said, "You are switching to the French horn. Your brother and you play the same cornet and your folks cannot afford two, so starting Monday you will play the school-owned French horn. Goodbye.")

Before I could even look at the music, he said, "You will play in a woodwind quintet, a French horn quartet, and a solo at Music Festival in the spring. Start practicing over the holidays." Mr. Baker did not do two-way conversation very well.

I got up to leave and then he said quietly, "I need a favor for tomorrow's performances. You know that (he named two of my fellow senior friends) cannot carry a tune. They are so far off that half the chorus is out of tune. I am going to ask them to just mouth the words. When I tell them, I want them to know that you are also going to mouth the words. If you are included, they will not feel as bad. Sing the carols, but that is all."

I felt a great sense of relief as I agreed to do it, because I did not want to screw up, but I liked his thinking that I could help them feel better about it. There is something gallant about "taking one for the team" or in this case "the chorus."

Before the matinee performance, Mr. Baker rearranged the bass section so that I was between the other two offending voices.

"So, are we really that bad?" one of them asked.

"It's no big deal. He knows his business."

The other friend said, "I can never tell my mother. She is so thrilled."

Finally I said, "Look, this is OK. We can sing the carols, just do it quietly. Don't make a peep during the 'Hallelujah Chorus' at the end. That's where we kill it. We'll practice during the matinee and really look good tonight."

Mr. Baker moved down from the stage to his position on a stand on the auditorium floor. There he directed the choir, separated by the piano and large arrangements of pine boughs all along the front of the stage. He had surprised everyone by unveiling a remarkable 10-foot-high rendition of the Savior, painted by an eccentric and admired local artist, Minerva Teichert of Cokeville, Wyoming. The portrait hung at center stage behind the choir. Only years later, after the renowned Mrs. Teichert's death, did we come to know and appreciate the truly distinguished and famous artistic master who had lived among us.

The 1958 Montpelier High School Christmas Cantata had three "lip-sync" basses. We kind of got into it and really worked on expression and timing. We did not even bother to sing the carols.

About three-fourths of the way through the evening concert, during "Silent Night," it hit me. "Mr. Baker thinks I am as bad as these other guys. Why else would he ask me to 'mouth-the-words' if I had any hope? Mr. Baker had conned me!" Actually the chorus did sound better without us, but I felt duped.

A minute later, I whispered to my friends and pointed to the final line on the last page of the score.

So as the chorus went through each of the "King of Kings" and "Lord of Lords," we mouthed the words with considerable expression and some degree of passion. After the last "Forever and Ever," and one more round of "King of Kings" and "Lord of Lords," we prepared ourselves for the final run of "Hallelujahs."

With Juliana Hayes pounding the piano so hard it was jumping and Mr. Baker working himself into a frenzy with his baton, everyone (but three) singing at the top of their lungs. All the others gathered themselves for the climax.

The three of us glanced at each other and joined in with total gusto for the final, "Hal-le-luuuuu-JAH!"

Juliana continued hammering, the choir held the note, and with baton poised to descend with a final swoop, Mr. Baker glared in our direction. I sheepishly shrugged my shoulders. He almost smiled as his baton finally circled to a conclusion.

Thunderous applause filled the auditorium while the heavy burgundy velvet curtains closed. When they re-opened for final bows, everyone smiled and waved, but I was long gone into the December night.

"Hal-le-luuuuuuuuu-JAH!"

ADDENDUM

In 1963 Wesley Baker moved from Montpelier to Boise where he became a representative for the Idaho Teacher's Association. His departure was a tragedy for our little southeastern Idaho community. A few years later, I made a point to visit him while on business in Boise.

I regret that he never said anything about the last note of the "Hallelujah Chorus," but he did chew me out for playing John Bissegger's four-note solo in the District Music Festival. We were playing in our French horn quartet and John, a freshman, hesitated, so I just played the notes.

We were given a top grade and Mr. Baker let me have it in no uncertain terms about honesty. (However, he forgave me enough to accompany me on my French horn solo and I received a top score—obviously because of his accompaniment.)

When I stopped by his office in Boise, it was weird—there was no piano, no sheet music and no music stand, not even a pile of records or a radio. He was out of context and the conversation was about my career and family.

As I left, he asked, "Do you ever play the horn?" I said, "No, Sir. I do not own one." "That is too bad," he lamented.

In 2007, when I left Deep Springs College as president, friends there presented me with a French horn. Mr. Baker would be most disappointed if he were to hear me play today.

Lynn Skinner, a fellow MHS friend and professor of music at the University of Idaho, frequently visited with Mr. Baker. He related to me that when Wes Baker became elderly and frail, suffering somewhat from dementia, his daughter or a grandchild often came to the assisted care facility to sit with him at a piano. There, in beautiful duets, his hands connected to his memory and those fingers magically came to life. I wish I could have witnessed that.

Dad and Ross prior to departing for Great Lakes LDS Mission, 1960

Elder Ross Peterson and other Montpelier missionaries in Great Lakes area (*clockwise from top left*) Ross, Richard Dayton, Bruce Arnell, Bob Wigington, Jerry Bissegger, Sister Mary Ann Jones, Dean Swenson. East Lansing, Michigan, 1962

12

Christmas Away from Home

There is a rhythm as a train's heavy steel wheels roll across the thin space that separates each rail from the next one. Mile after mile, the train sounds the same as it makes its way over the rails headed west. After two years-plus in the service of the Lord as LDS missionaries, a small group of us were headed home shortly before Christmas in 1962.

Initially we climbed aboard an old passenger train headed west out of Fort Wayne, Indiana and stopped in Chicago. Following a four-hour layover, Allen Hackworth and I left those headed toward Utah and we boarded City of Portland, the Union Pacific's deluxe streamliner, bound for Idaho. As we skimmed along the rails from Chicago, we abandoned our purchased seats and raced to the dome car and stayed there.

One of many things learned as missionaries was that food and sleep were not necessities of life for any twenty-hour period. Watching America roll by might be a once-in-a-lifetime opportunity, so we settled in for the journey.

It had been twenty-six months since I left from Salt Lake City. Now Streamliner U.P. 105 headed for the Rockies and would stop in my hometown, Montpelier, Idaho. The fact that it was soon Christmas heightened our excitement to get home.

The ride was smooth and the stops frequent; we could see the lighted trappings of Christmas at every station along the way. As the train rolled across Illinois and then over the Mississippi River into Iowa, I thought of pioneers a century earlier who had made this trek in wagons or pushing carts under duress. What ultimately took them five months, we were going to do in two days.

Iowa's snow-covered cornfields were left behind at the Missouri, and we had a pretty lengthy stop in Omaha. The Nebraska portion took all night and by the time we climbed into southern Wyoming, it was morning. The whistle-stops were in Cheyenne, Laramie, Medicine Bow, Rawlins, Rock Springs, and Green River—where the U.P. crews from Montpelier engineered every train headed west.

There was no sleep nor desire to sleep, so memories and plans jammed into a roadblock *in my brain and the time passed more and more slowly as I gazed out at Wyoming's sagebrush and wind-swept high plains.*

I laughed aloud as I recalled my feelings about two years earlier, in October 1960, as I left for a two-year stint as a missionary. No dates, no school, no movies, no baseball, and letters only once a week.

I was not really prepared nor was I particularly worried. There had been plenty of goofy characters from my hometown who had said yes to the same call and were sent across the world. They and the Church had both survived. Besides, five of us from the Montpelier Stake were going at the same time to the same place, the Great Lakes Mission. In fact, three of my friends had been through twelve years of school with me, so homesickness was not a real threat.

Richard Dayton, the other person from our stake, was from Cokeville, Wyoming and was sad all night as the Denver and Rio Grande made its way east to Denver. He had a serious girlfriend and prayed that she would wait, but none of us comforted him.

It was common knowledge that few girlfriends waited, so there was no need to whine or panic. Bob Wigington just told him, "She won't wait." (She did) We agreed, and although armed with addresses and stamps, we knew it could be as scary to have girls wait as to have them dump us. Good grief, we were all of nineteen and three of the five thought they had already found their eternal companions.

Our group, nine total, had a four-hour layover in Denver and wandered toward the city, but we worried about our suitcases and two years' worth of new suits, white shirts, topcoats, dress hats, scriptures, socks, and underwear. When we boarded the Burlington Route's Zephyr to Chicago, a bit of anxiety crept into my mind.

My concern was Jerry Bissegger, who had contracted polio when we were high school sophomores. Now, four years later, with his legs braced and hand crutches on his arms, he too was going for two years. We had been together as college freshmen at Utah State, and in the winter it was really hard for him to get around. I knew he was worried about his widowed mother and three siblings, but his faith and commitment were real.

My faith was pretty untested and I worried more about money. So when someone suggested we get a sleeping berth for the second night, I declined, but we talked Jerry into doing it. I just stared into the night all the way to Lincoln, Nebraska. When we got to Chicago, we chose to stay in the huge train station until the Rock Island Line left for Fort Wayne, Indiana. It took us nearly three days to get from Salt Lake City to Fort Wayne, our mission headquarters.

Now we were heading home. For a number of reasons, including toe surgery, I stayed in the Midwest until well into December of 1962, so Jerry, Bob, Richard, and Dean Swenson were all home before I left Indiana. The mission president had called my folks and asked their permission to have me stay longer and also asked them if I had health insurance. They must have answered "certainly" to the extended stay and "no" to the insurance.

That led him to the decision to have my infected ingrown toenails operated on to have the nail beds scraped on the Church's insurance. My feet were still in need of twice-daily soaks in epsom salts when I left Fort Wayne on my way home to Idaho.

When we got to Chicago, Elder Hackworth and I threw our stuff into a locker, caught a bus to Lakeshore Drive, and in a windy sleet storm raced to the Museum of Natural History, an observatory, and a museum. We got back to the station with five minutes to spare, checked our luggage, and nabbed the seats in the dome car. Many thousands of Chicago Christmas lights were turned on in the daytime. They made us feel great about getting home for Christmas. We did not talk much for the rest of the trip.

As usual my parents had a job for me that would start the day after I got home, at the Burgoyne's store. The delightful, small, family-operated clothing and shoe store was owned by longtime friends.

Dad always made sure we had a job the day school was out in the spring. The Monday after high school graduation, I had started a great summer job at a ready-mix concrete plant and worked until the day I left for college. The day after my last final in the spring, I started back at the concrete plant, Patton and Linton. It was a memorable summer because I worked with Dad and my brother Max. We played softball and for the first summer in many, I did not have an addition to my police record.

So I knew that the morning after I arrived in Montpelier from my mission, I'd put on my worn-out suit and work through the Christmas season and then go back to college. That was fine with me. There was no doubt that I needed money. I'd be leaving for school right after the new year. Then I thought of my financial situation. Dad had broken his elbow the first winter I was in Ohio and could not work, so $80 a month sent to me was a bit steep for the family budget.

We dipped into my college savings and I also bought an old 1953 Ford for $185 to replace the dilapidated Plymouth that died one day on a street in Akron, Ohio. It was a great move on my part because it guaranteed me a car for the rest of my mission and I never again wore out suit pants on the seat of a bike. Then when the church bought thousands of Rambler Americans, I drove new cars.

The conductor shouted "Green River!" It was only three in the afternoon, but already growing dark. In three hours I would be home, and Christmas would be like the first eighteen in my life, not like the two I had just experienced.

I chuckled aloud as I recalled Christmas of 1960 in Akron, Ohio, and the next year in Lansing, Michigan. Maybe I changed a lot during those two years. I certainly felt that 21 years old was a lot older than 19. My hand rubbed across my scruffy chin to document the reality of aging.

I had arrived in Akron in late October and with my companion spent the next few weeks pounding the pavement, trying to get anyone to invite us back for discussions and lessons. In retrospect, it was all about an education in life. Rejection was frequent, prayers more fervent, and homesickness one slammed-door away.

There were fun times, such as seeing the couple embracing through the window as we knocked on the door. Like a deer caught in the headlights, she opened the door and I said, "We're ministers, may we come in?" She said, "Yes," and I began the introduction: "I am Elder Peterson and this is Elder Bake. You'd be—?" "Wanda Jones," she said. I turned to the man. "And you'd be Mr. Jones?" He stammered and muttered, "No, I'm the milkman."

There was also the time we had out our flannel board (on which adhere cut-out figures and names) and were really feeling the spirit as we taught a young couple in his parents' living room. Suddenly the man's mother came dancing between the flannel board and the attentive couple. With her platinum blond hair swinging from side to side, she sashayed in front of us. She wore only a pair of bright lavender high-heeled shoes. I bowed quickly, stared at the shoes, and said, "Let us pray."

We were delivered from temptation by her angry husband and son. The new elder with me admitted on the way to our apartment that she was the first naked woman he had ever seen. Then with a tearful voice, "Why did it have to be her?" My feelings exactly.

By early December we were not setting the world on fire with converts and Elder Bake was getting nervous about why the Lord had not blessed us. We studied, prayed, fasted every Friday, and tracted door-to-door. Hey, Christmas was coming. Who had time or interest in listening to door-to-door salesmen disguised as ministers?

Elder Bake was convinced we were not working hard enough or exhibiting enough faith. He chastised me for light-mindedness when I used my deepest voice through the air vent and tried to convince our neighbor, Mrs. Grubb, to "Join the Mormon Church." I blamed the 1950 puke-green Plymouth with the left rear fender missing, pork and beans can as a gas cap, and floorboard on the driver's side rusted out. By the time we got that thing going each day, I had lost more religion than in a month of milking cows.

One day in southeast Akron a cheerful young housewife, filled with Christmas spirit, let us in. Because it was very cold, we relaxed and talked about being away from home. Mrs. McCallister took mercy on us and invited us to eat Christmas dinner with her family. A few days later we returned and gave the first gospel lesson to her and her husband. They liked the idea of studying the scriptures, prayer, and were not shocked when we told them about Joseph Smith.

They again invited us for Christmas dinner and Elder Bake said, "Yes, thank you. We would be honored." This was good because we could now count Christmas hours as working hours and those weekly reports seemed important.

The McCallisters agreed to hear the second lesson in three days, only a week before Christmas. No one else invited us to Christmas dinner, so we felt that finally our prayers were answered. We looked forward to a great time at Christmas.

Any home-cooked meal sounded fantastic. Bake made powdered milk, powdered mashed potatoes, powdered orange juice, and powdered eggs. His oatmeal made the memories of my mother's, which made me gag in my youth, really sound good. No wonder I looked forward to fasting on Fridays. And he complained about my extravagance when I cooked real food and not Spam or other World War II surplus rations.

When we went back three days later, the chill was on. Friends, ministers, co-workers, parents, and the devil had marshaled their talents and we could not get the Book of Mormon lesson out of Joseph Smith's bedroom in 1823. The metal plates never got found or translated into another testament for Jesus Christ. So with no prayer, small talk, or friendliness, the evening deteriorated as they talked about polygamy, blood atonement, and other doctrinal issues that had never made their way into our ears as we progressed through Seminary.

As we prepared to leave, Elder Bake asked, "What time should we come on Christmas?" I tried to kick him under the coffee table. She looked at her husband, he at her, shrugs and scowls were exchanged, and then she said, "We will eat at one."

When we left I said, "Let's cancel. No way do they want us around." He responded, "This is their only chance and they did invite us. No one else has." We argued for the rest of the week. One night he prayed that the Lord would soften my heart and pretty much laid it out to Heavenly

Father that my attitude was why Akron, Ohio's citizens were not opening their souls and doors.

On Christmas morning I just prayed that, whatever happened that day, we would "get home safely and the stupid car would start." I opened my presents. The box of homemade cookies from the Montpelier Third Ward Beehives were all crumbs. Two girls vying for my affection sent cookies and a fruitcake, also crumbs. Then I opened the gifts from home— socks, a shirt, and more underwear. I made my allowed collect phone call home, faked being really upbeat, and then got very sad.

It was one of those gray, snowy mornings that kept all the pollution from Akron's numerous tire plants down close to the ground and in our noses, throats, and lungs. My entire family, but me, was at home. Then we prayed and went to the McCallisters!

There is a difference between an awkward atmosphere and a tense one, filled with negative vibes. The hour of Christmas dinner was beyond all of the above. We gave some gifts to their children, ate a pretty good meal and utterly failed at all attempts at small talk. They finally admitted that their family was coming at six o'clock for the real meal and they felt bad that none of us knew how to be honest. We agreed.

Then Elder Bake suggested something really wise and healing. He asked if we could read the Nativity story in the second chapter of Luke before leaving. That touch of reality made all of us feel good about being together. We never saw them again, even though we thanked them when leaving, wrote a thank-you note, and tried to stop by a couple of times. No wonder Joseph the Carpenter had to put his family in the stable—no one really likes strangers at Christmas.

As the train left Green River heading toward Montpelier, I came back to the present when someone shouted my name. A crew of Montpelier railroad workers, including Max Lyons, Mel Smith, and some others I recognized got on the nearly full train to deadhead back to Montpelier. We exchanged pleasantries, and I thought it was ironic that two of the first people I met from home were Max and Mel. Dad and I home-taught Mel, but he never went to church. For two years I had been trying to bring souls into the gospel, and here were friends from home who still needed to hear the word.

However, I resisted the temptation to preach and just invited them to sacrament meeting when I would report on my two-year sojourn. I made my way out of the dome as we approached Kemmerer. I jumped onto the station platform and noticed the sky behind us had darkened. It was really cold and I could tell we were getting close to home.

My second Christmas away had been in East Lansing, Michigan. By then, the girls were not writing or sending cookies. My expectations were very low. I think the Beehives were convinced I would remain in the Midwest, so there were no crumbs from them. I had been transferred from Lancaster, Ohio to Michigan on Thanksgiving weekend. I picked up a new robin-egg-blue Rambler in Fort Wayne and drove north to my new assignment.

A few weeks later, right before Christmas, Gifford Price, my companion, got dumped by his college sweetheart. He called her every day until I threatened to disconnect the phone. In that atmosphere he made a decision that we had to go meet all the members and seek their help in finding prospects.

Since most of the members were affiliated with Michigan State University, this meant going into the homes of professors and graduate students, and seeking their friends. We, meaning all missionaries, were already considered a bit aggressive and too persistent. Some members were embarrassed as they heard us talk about baptism in the first lesson.

When we went to the home of Gaurth Hansen, the chair of the Biochemistry Department, he let us have it with both barrels. We were chastised for every sin or suspected sin of every missionary in the past thirty years since he had served his own mission in New England during the Depression.

After about a half-hour of his constructive analysis of how to make friends and let them make their own decisions, I said, "We have to go. May we have a word of prayer? I'll offer it." Before anyone realized, I had breached a code of conduct relative to who was in charge in their own home. I prayed, "Heavenly Father, we thank thee for the gracious hospitality of Sister Hansen and we ask thee to bless her and her family. Please bless us to get home safely. In the name of Jesus Christ, Amen."

Before we could open our eyes, Anna Lou Hansen said, "Thank you very much. Would you like to join us for Christmas dinner?" Now, Gaurth Hansen had not only a sharp tongue, but also laser vision. He tried to stare through his wife and she just smiled. "We'd be honored," we said in unison. Then we began to visit and I talked to their three sons, Roger, Ted, and Lars. Before we left their home, I had established an important connection with the Hansens.

They were from Cache Valley, Utah where my grandparents had moved after they sold their farm in Bear Lake County. The Hansens' best young-married friends were Perth and Arvila Poulsen, my aunt and uncle. In the Mormon world, if you talk to anyone long enough you'll find you are either related to them or know someone who is related. We laughed as we got into our new 1961 Nash Rambler American and drove to the next house.

On Christmas Eve morning, we got a phone call at 6 a.m. from a new missionary in Detroit. He whispered, "My companion smokes and he says he is going home." I immediately called one of the missionary leaders in Detroit and said, "Meet us at their apartment at 8:30."

We dressed quickly and agreed on the strategy for keeping the guy in the fold. He had wonderful people skills and worked hard. Unfortunately, he had never been able to completely quit smoking. We had been hiding it from the leaders for quite some time. His girlfriend and parents had put pressure on him to serve and he went, like me, before the LDS Church had perfected the worthiness interview. His girlfriend had found another and he just wanted out of there. Three of us spent the day with this young man.

In a weird way, it was a great Christmas experience. We relaxed and visited about home, school, girlfriends, and then the Savior. I tried to convince him that if he quit smoking for the rest of his mission, he would do a lot of good for the Savior. We went over the Sermon on the Mount, the Last Supper, a few parables, and the Garden of Gethsemane.

We went to McDonald's for lunch and he bought us all the one dollar special—

cheeseburger, fries, drink and shake. That Christmas Eve day was fun.

Then he said, "Let's pool our cash and buy some things for the families we teach." For the rest of the day we gave poorly wrapped but essential small gifts to children of Detroit. Making sure we had enough to buy gas to get back to Lansing, we dumped the rest of our change in a Salvation Army pot outside a Sears department store.

As we left, the wavering Elder agreed that he would call me or his leader in Detroit every time he got the urge to smoke and he said he could make it until next August. We left Detroit and got back to Lansing by midnight.

The noontime dinner the next day was easy. We had slept in and neither one of us had a lot of gifts, but the phone calls were great. The Hansens also invited Dick Swensen's family to dinner. There were enough children to play with. The earlier tension was long gone. The children took turns reading about the birth of the Savior and it felt very comfortable.

Maybe Gaurth was right about slowing down and letting people make their own decisions in their own good time. We might have had a totally different experience with the McCallisters had we been more patient. The Hansens and the Swensens became lifelong friends.

In all honesty, compared with all my Christmases at home, those two away taught me a lot about Christmas. We had no trees, no decorations, few gifts—just food and time that we should have used in service to others. In retrospect, we could have served better during the holidays, but I also realized, as the train passed through Cokeville, Wyoming and we followed my beloved Bear River toward home, you cannot change the past. You just learn from it and try to do better.

As we entered Bear Lake Valley, fog engulfed the train. The "City of Portland" never slowed, but it seemed like it took forever to get from Pegram through Dingle, north to Montpelier. I loved trains and I wished Dad still worked for the Union Pacific. There was nothing better than a free railroad pass and a steady paycheck to balance the losses on the farm. Ohio and Michigan were both cold and humid, but it was fitting that I re-entered Bear Lake Valley in a foggy below-zero evening like so many in my past. Winter and fog were synonymous. Whether milking or playing basketball or helping feed the cattle, a Bear Lake winter was in a class of its own.

Finally the train slowed as it entered Montpelier from the south. It passed over the crossing to our ranch, and stopped with the engine by the freight house. The dome car was just north of the tiny red brick station. In the fog, I could barely make out a few figures standing near the station platform. The Christmas lights along Main Street disappeared into the fog within a block and the blue spruce trees in the median four blocks away, draped in Christmas lights, were not visible.

I put my tattered overcoat over my threadbare suit, cinched up my tie, and put the Hamburg dress hat on for the last time. I would never wear the white shirt with frayed collar again. Like so much of what I brought home, its destiny was the rag bin. I told my traveling companion goodbye and quickly walked from the dome car down into the train toward the door.

Max Lyons said, "Go first."

I had not shaved, showered, or changed clothes for three days. I waited as the conductor opened the door and placed the portable step between the train and platform. Mother, Dad, Reed, and Brent were standing on the platform. Our neighbors, Norma Wigington, who had been ravaged by arthritis to the point of being hardly recognizable, and her daughter Nell, were standing behind the four members of my Montpelier family.

I broke free from the door, stared at Reed and Brent, who had each grown half a foot, shook their hands, slapped them on the back, embraced my parents and muttered, "I'm home for Christmas."

My dad kept punching me on the arm and my mother cried. Reed and Brent picked up the suitcase and the blue metal chest that had accompanied me throughout the two years. Mother said, "Everyone will be here by Sunday."

The streamliner pulled away through the dense fog, and I thought, "I really need to sleep before Christmas."

"City of Portland" Domeliner brought Ross back home to Montpelier, 1962

ABOUT THE AUTHOR

F Ross Peterson was raised on a small farm in Montpelier, Idaho. His family learned through the Great Depression and World War II values of sacrifice, cooperation, and thriftiness from their parents, Raymond and Zora Peterson, who married in 1933. Ross was a multi-sport athlete and student body president at Montpelier High School. He received a degree in History from Utah State University in 1965 and a PhD in American Studies from Washington State University in 1968. After three years teaching at the University of Texas at Arlington, he returned to USU in 1971.

With his great passion for teaching, he has served as Professor of History at Utah State University specializing in Recent American History with an emphasis on the Civil Rights Movement and its efforts to achieve an inclusive nation. Throughout his career he has influenced the lives of countless students. From 1976 to 1986, he chaired the Department of History and Geography. In 1986, he received a challenge grant from the National Endowment for the

Humanities to establish the Mountain West Center for Regional Studies, where he served as director for over a decade.

Dr. Peterson left USU in 2004 to become president of Deep Springs College in eastern California. During his tenure at Deep Springs, his devotion to possibilities for students expanded dramatically as the philosophy of academics, labor, and self-governance influenced young lives at that unique college.

In 2007 he returned to USU as Vice President for Advancement and helped conduct the university's first comprehensive fundraising campaign. Through the efforts of the Advancement team, the university's endowment and scholarships grew dramatically. This position allowed him to reconnect with students and friends from throughout the world.

He has also served on many volunteer boards including the Utah Humanities Council and the Utah State Board of History. In 1998, Governor Michael Leavitt and the Utah Humanities Council presented Peterson with the Governor's Outstanding Humanist Award for the state of Utah. Peterson and his wife, Mary Kay, edited, *Dialogue: A Journal of Mormon Thought* for a five-year term.

Peterson has published numerous books on Western American topics. His great love is teaching and he has been honored to be the recipient of numerous teaching awards from Utah State University. In 1978-79, Victoria University in New Zealand granted him a Fulbright lectureship to teach African American history. He was named the Wayne Aspinall Chair in American Western History at Colorado Mesa University, Grand Junction, Colorado in 2015.

Ross and Mary Kay, also from Montpelier, Idaho are the parents of three sons and have eleven grandchildren and five great grandsons. They live in the same home in River Heights, Cache County, that they bought when they came to Utah in 1971. It is less than ten minutes from Utah State University and any place they need or want to be.

A good life.

Also by F. Ross Peterson

. *A History of Bear Lake Pioneers*, editor
. *Prophet Without Honor: Glen H. Taylor and the Fight For American Liberalism*
. *Idaho: A Bicentennial History*
. "Politics and Protest" in *The Oxford History of the American West* with Michael P. Malone
. *A History of Cache County*
. *Ogden City: Its Governmental Legacy* with Robert Parson
. "Confronting the Desert" in *The Snake: The Plain and Its People*
. *A History of the Central Utah Project* with Robert Parson and Craig Fuller

GLOSSARY

Members of The Church of Jesus Christ of Latter-day Saints have a jargon all their own. Most residents in Montpelier, Idaho were and are Church members. They are also called Latter-day Saints, LDS, or Mormons, from the Book of Mormon. The following terms are sprinkled throughout this book.

Beehive — The youngest of several groups of girls who meet each week for spiritual and social activities.

Book of Mormon — A book of scripture considered another witness for Jesus Christ.

Bishop — Volunteer leader of a ward

Eternal Companion — Members are encouraged to marry in a Temple, where they may be "sealed" to live as husband and wife with their families forever.

Fast offering — Members fast once a month. Money they would have spent on food is instead donated to the poor.

Missionaries — Members who serve in one of hundreds of missions; primarily young men for two years and young women for eighteen months.

Priesthood — Worthy males twelve years and older are eligible to receive the priesthood, the power and authority to act for our Heavenly Father.

Primary — The children's organization, ages 3 – 12 of the LDS church.

Relief Society — The women's auxiliary of the LDS church.

Seminary — A weekday religious program for students of high school age.

Sacrament meeting — The most important of three meetings members attend each Sunday.

Stake — A group of wards or, in a mission, a group of branches.

Temple — A "House of the Lord," where worthy members make sacred covenants as they participate in the highest ordinances of God.

Tithing — Members of all ages are encouraged to donate 10 percent of their income to the Church to finance its worldwide activities.

Ward — Congregations are divided geographically into wards or branches.

Ward teachers — A former program in which two male members called upon assigned families each month to render service.

Index

A

B

H

Hackworth, Allen 161, 165
Hansen, Anna Lou 174
Hansen, Gaurth 173, 174, 176
Hayes, Juliana 156
Henrie, Doug 99, 100, 101
Holmes, Sarah 4, 37 – 43, 45, 46, 47
Hooker's 40, 51, 120
Hymas, Virginia 28

I

Irving, George 24
Irving, LaPriel 28

J

Jaussi, J. L. 83, 84, 89, 91
Jensen, Elmer 55
Jones, Mary Ann 160
Jones, Wanda 167

K

Keetch, Beverly 31
Kimball 81, 92

L

Larsen, Ron 63
Larsen, Uncle Leon 8
Leavitt, Michael 182
Lyons, Delano 143

M

Mark 3, 7, 19, 20, 21
McCallisters 169, 171, 176
Meiners, Miss 136, 138, 142, 143
Messerly, Eddie 25, 34, 55
Messerly, Grant 4, 24, 25, 27, 32, 33, 129, 151